"From the moment of our first breath, ... arduous journey of mental conditioning, ...dual and social selves. In *How to Be a Spiritual* ..., Jac O'Keeffe astutely guides us how to leave this conditioning and its endless searching behind for a new life beyond boundaries, beyond limitations. In such a life, each moment is lived not by conditions of the mind but rather by your inner spiritual nature, which guides you in an ongoing and ever-blossoming transformation of openness to and participation in life itself. Freedom for its own sake and authenticity are the hallmarks of a life lived free of the conditioned self."

—**Paul J. Mills, PhD**, professor in the department of family medicine and public health, director of the Center of Excellence for Research and Training in Integrative Health, and chief of the Behavioral Medicine Division at the University of California, San Diego; and director of research at The Chopra Foundation

"Jac O'Keeffe is one of the rare presenters of prior-to, without, or beyond consciousness and non-duality. This provides a context making her unique as both a teacher and educator."

NO LONGER PROPERTY OF
SEATTLE PUBLIC LIBRARY

—**Stephen H. Wolinsky, PhD (Narayan)**, disciple of Sri Nisargadatta Maharaj

"Jac O'Keeffe has brilliantly deconstructed her own deep spiritual process to provide clear, simple guidelines and practices for all others who long for psychological and spiritual freedom. She provides tools to prepare us for living the deepest Truth, free of personal clinging to false identities. Using her own internal journey as a template, she offers a path to freedom and teaches us how to change neural pathways in the brain, freeing consciousness from the conditioned restraints and limitations caused by self-referencing thought and emotion. This unique, modern book on non-dual awakening and beyond will become a classic for those who seek realization."

—**Bonnie Greenwell, PhD**, transpersonal psychotherapist and non-dual teacher; and author of *The Kundalini Guide*, *The Awakening Guide*, and *When Spirit Leaps*

"*How to Be a Spiritual Rebel* illuminates a clear and practical pathway for breaking out of automated mental patterns, and finally living an authentic life. With fierce honesty, courage, and palpable care for her reader, Jac shares potent turning points in her own journey into practices that will serve any lover of the Truth to cut through subtle deception and find their way to Freedom."

—**Miranda Macpherson**, contemporary spiritual teacher, author of *The Way of Grace* and *Boundless Love*, and founder of OneSpirit Interfaith Foundation (UK) and the Living Grace Sangha

"*How to Be a Spiritual Rebel* offers potent truths about how mindfulness and compassion can bring greater happiness, health, and freedom into our lives."

—**Shauna Shapiro, PhD**, professor in the department of counseling psychology at Santa Clara University, and author of *Good Morning, I Love You*

"In *How to Be a Spiritual Rebel*, Jac O'Keeffe provides a deeply wise, kind, and practical guide to untangling yourself from limiting beliefs and habits, and points to the intrinsic freedom of the heart that is available to us all."

—**Hugh Byrne, PhD**, senior teacher with the Insight Meditation Community of Washington, and author of *The Here-and-Now Habit*

HOW TO
be a
SPIRITUAL
REBEL

A DOGMA-FREE GUIDE TO
BREAKING ALL THE RULES &
FINDING FEARLESS FREEDOM

JAC O'KEEFFE

NON-DUALITY PRESS
An Imprint of New Harbinger Publications

Publisher's Note

This publication is designed to provide accurate and authoritative information in regard to the subject matter covered. It is sold with the understanding that the publisher is not engaged in rendering psychological, financial, legal, or other professional services. If expert assistance or counseling is needed, the services of a competent professional should be sought.

Distributed in Canada by Raincoast Books

Copyright © 2019 by Jac O'Keeffe
       Non-Duality Press
       An imprint of New Harbinger Publications, Inc.
       5674 Shattuck Avenue
       Oakland, CA 94609
       www.newharbinger.com

Cover design by Amy Shoup

Acquired by Elizabeth Hollis Hansen

All Rights Reserved

FSC
www.fsc.org
MIX
Paper from
responsible sources
FSC® C011935

Library of Congress Cataloging-in-Publication Data on file

Printed in the United States of America

21   20   19

10   9   8   7   6   5   4   3   2   1   First Printing

Contents

PART 4: The Influence of Pain

PART 5: Breaking Free from Limitations

PART 6: Bring It On!

PART 7: Bursting the Spiritual Bubble

PART 8: It Comes Together in the End

Introduction

Our family business was a dairy farm. It was an efficiently run endeavor, not least because of the wonderful, fertile pastures of North Cork, Ireland. A dairy farm is labor intensive, commanding all hands on-deck for at least ten months of the year. The family comprised of my parents, five older sisters, and a sheepdog. We were raised with a strong work ethic; cows require milking twice a day until midway into the last trimester of each pregnancy. Then came calving season kicking off in mid-January. During the six weeks that followed, the farm shifted focus to accommodate a bovine maternity ward and neonatal clinic. The population increased daily with newborn calves that, once taken from their mothers, had to be taught how to drink milk from a bucket. Cows hollered for their newborns, and my father would say, "She'll forget her calf in a few days." I wasn't so sure.

When we started going out with boys (who had to have a car due to our rural location) as teenagers, we would find a note on the kitchen table when we came home late at night. The note would ask us to check on an animal that was calving. I enjoyed getting a pair of rubber boots for a date, bringing him to the back stall, watching his horrified face as he saw, for the first time, a calf's front hooves (when all was well) protruding from the birth canal. I had no interest in boys who were of farming stock. I wanted a ticket out of cow dung and milking machines for as long as I can remember. Although I must admit being reared on a farm had many romantic moments: gathering bales of straw, picking wild blackberries, and the gift of living in the rhythm of nature.

The flip side was there also. My father was angry. He had a short fuse and believed that violence was to be administered to children and animals alike. Beatings were frequent and arbitrary. My mother stepped back into the shadows when he was physically violent, perhaps to protect herself. Later, as adults, each of us six girls had to face and process traumatic experiences from childhood. Some of us delved deeper into therapy than others. All in all, we now function moderately well as a family, and there remains much wisdom and maturation to be gleaned from healing our past.

When I left home for college as a young adult, I discovered that students were eligible for free psychotherapy. Within a week of learning this, I began therapy and continued with regularity until graduation. After college I continued with therapy, moving from psychotherapy to rebirthing, past life regression, voice work, sweat lodges, and plant medicine (both in the Amazonian jungle and in Ireland), along with a multitude of other modalities of varying efficacies. My journey continued far beyond finding peace with my father. Through these explorations, I found tools that helped me answer the fundamental questions that had been with me as long as I can remember. *What am I doing here? Am I here at all? What's it all for? Does purpose matter?* These questions led me to spirituality, and by my early thirties that was my singular focus. I was guided, and often driven towards, something that I could not glimpse until later. Sometimes curiosity or a desire to be happy motivates our spiritual growth. Other times our motivation is neither personal nor logical. In these cases we can feel compelled by another force, by an innate impulsion that we intuitively know we can and must trust.

During my spiritual explorations, meditation served as my anchor while my external life changed in every way imaginable. Abandoning the home I had set up with my husband and my successful healing practice that had a six-month waiting list, I went towards sunlight. I wanted to know more. What was the light that is referred to in healing and new age modalities? I decided I should start with what I truly knew and understood light to be—and that was physical sunlight.

I moved to a campsite in Spain, and after three months of concerted meditation, the next step became clear. I resolved to follow an inner urge (that to the best of my knowledge did not originate in my mind) and take whatever step presented next. I was never shown two steps at the same time. I would take one step, and eventually the next would be given. Then I would take that step. And so on. Within two years I was in the south of India, focusing only on my spiritual practice. Apart from meditating and chanting, my waking hours were dedicated to identifying every piece of my conditioning I could, and breaking its authority by challenging my norms and expectations. I broke every personal law and social rule that had questionable validity. I wanted to know who I would become if I stopped obeying my shoulds and shouldn'ts, if I no longer fulfilled my expectations of myself. *What would happen if I became the person in my past or my present whom I judge negatively?* I broke all the rules, and I learned through experience. I wondered: *What would happen if I had no habitual reference points? If I no longer supported my thoughts, my beliefs, and my socially-ingrained values, would I have a personal identity?* These are lofty questions, but I've never been interested in theory. My research was, and continues to be, action-based. I spent very long periods of time in silence, external silence, and eventually internal silence. For a long time, there was nothing but silence.

Then one day I became acutely aware of a change taking place in my brain. There had been copious spiritual experiences, most of which are forgotten now, but not this one. This particular event marks a significant point of growth on my path and is further discussed in Chapter 6. I was in the shower, which where I was staying in southern India meant self-administering jugs of cold water drawn from a bucket of non-potable water. In this moment I noticed that something was happening in my brain. There was a sensation mostly localized deep within the upper left side of my head. It felt like something in my brain was tearing and breaking apart. It wasn't physically painful. I experienced it as simply a sensation. I had an uncanny feeling that something familiar was slipping away, coupled with an uncomfortable knowing that the change that was occurring would be permanent. I instantly came up with two scenarios; either an unusual spiritual experience was happening, or I was losing my mind. My trust in my ongoing process was so solid at that stage that both options were met with full acceptance. I was ready for whatever came next.

Many years later I learned that I had short-circuited my *self-referencing network*, which I have since seen defined as the *Default*

Mode Network (DMN). The personality of "Jac," the Irish woman, repositioned itself as an outpost of an inner divine nature that is common to all. I had tipped the balance to where a meditative state was the new normal. My attention had anchored itself within me, in an inner sanctuary of stillness and truth. After this, all thoughts stopped for two years. I continued to participate in the world, but did so against the backdrop of peace and stillness, instead of the self-talk and internal commentary that used to be there. This sense of peace and stillness has remained with me ever since.

In recent years neuroscience has started catching up with facts that I learned from my spiritual path. It's an exciting time we live in, when science can offer vocabulary for and new ways to help us understand the changes that one experiences on a spiritual journey. What I know to be true is starting to be mirrored in neuroscience. What I know to be Truth stands apart from any phenomenal explanation. Both what is true and Truth are accessible to you. I recommend viewing science as a support, an aid to understanding and categorizing what we know from our shared experience. To date, the wisdom of our internal knowing is still much more profound than the reaches of science, and, though I sometimes draw on the insight of science, your experience will be your guide in the book that follows.

In my work as a spiritual teacher I address each student individually. Together we explore and identify inhibitors to spiritual awakening. Each path is unique and, while certain issues are common to all, one also needs a tool kit for honest self-reflection and self-management. Skills in psychological introspection are equally as important as skills in meditation. Teachers who have not explored their own psychological vulnerabilities are susceptible to the abuse of power and exploitation of students for their own unaddressed needs. Our divine nature does not negate our human nature; unexamined belief systems compromise our human potential and obscure the intelligence of our divine nature. Any bona fide spiritual path means honoring both psychological and spiritual aspects of one's experience. Authentic awakening, an awakening that is fully integrated (embodied) in each moment, requires an honoring of both your divine and your human nature.

In *How to Be a Spiritual Rebel: A Dogma-Free Guide to Breaking All the Rules and Finding Fearless Freedom* I have selected the most common psychological issues that block students from spiritual growth and maturity. I encourage you to embrace both psychological and spiritual perspectives as one approach, so that you will be open to exploring whatever shows up as an inhibitor to your spiritual growth. Traditionally, the psychological approach is called the "indirect path," while withdrawing all attention from the mind is the "direct path." My work combines both approaches. Just like the gardener who knows which weeds to dig up by the roots and which can be covered with bark mulch, I recommend that you be open to understanding more about the subtle tricks of your mind. Some beliefs must be challenged, while others can be ignored. The chapters ahead will help you to cultivate the wisdom to know the difference.

I've worked as a spiritual teacher for over a decade, and it has been my privilege to see many students awaken. I hope that these same teachings, distilled here in this book, are even more accessible now that they have been enriched by recent scientific findings. I have no interest in drawing evidence from science that merely seems to fit my purposes. I see the tracks of science and spirituality in parallel, each has its own *raison d'être*. As a spiritual teacher my bias is to the inner knowing that is beyond evidence, time, and space. I give gratitude to science and scientists who can pave the way to a greater understanding. The evidence they find serves to relax your mind with understanding so that you might surrender to the depth of your own being and the ultimate fearless freedom that awaits. The words herein are simply signposts pointing the way.

PART 1

IN THE ABSENCE
OF COURAGE

CHAPTER 1

Freedom

This book helps you define and honor what you know to be authentic and true within you. I spent years honoring what I believed was authentic and true only to discover that I was supporting my own conditioned beliefs—sophisticated beliefs, but still just beliefs all the same. How do we get beyond beliefs so that you can access what is not an idea from your conditioned mind? How can you discern for yourself what is authentic and true? That's our journey. There is a place inside you that is deeper than the stream of thoughts produced by the conditioned mind. As you get more familiar with that place, it comes to feel like *you*. A place, no, it's not a *place*. But the word "place," clumsy as it is, must suffice to express something that is outside time and space, outside and beyond personal consciousness. Yet we know it intuitively once we are oriented in its direction. Words are very effective in helping us navigate the external, outer world that makes up the bulk of our life. Now I'm using the same material tools (words) to guide you through an immaterial territory that is simply not made of the same stuff.

How can I navigate you to what is deeper than your thoughts? Does the word "deeper" work? How can I be sure you can sense where I am pointing to when each person's path is entirely different? How I can satisfactorily explain in print what cannot be adequately conveyed in words? *I can't.* As I wrote this book, I made a concerted effort to try and avoid what has become spiritual jargon, but I have at times resorted to clichés to give direction and pointers that might be of use to you. Phrases like "look within" and "inner spiritual nature" are clichés. When you come across them in this book, try to set aside what you think they mean and instead feel into their meaning. In other words, discover what they mean to you in each moment by dropping your consciousness below your neck, into your torso. When you look inwardly towards your spiritual nature by sensing and feeling, rather than thinking, what I am talking about with these words will resonate inside you. This resonance is the gateway to freedom.

There is freedom when you are able to live your life each day in alignment with your own authentic, true nature. Playing safe ends, and manipulation stops. You no longer say and do things in order to forward your own subtle agenda. In my work I meet many people who meditate daily for years and still remain quite dysfunctional in their day-to-day lives and relationships. This book addresses how to end the conflict between your inner spiritual nature and how you think and act in life. Our goal is to attune your mind to your spiritual nature and to free up your actions so that you are honest and true to the core of your being. You are not done until you can walk and talk your deepest wisdom. Even then, ongoing growth and development continue. The spiritual path has no ultimate destination.

Early on my spiritual path I was in conflict. My culture and community advocated behavioral norms and guidelines, as all societies do, based on their values and traditions. From what I could see it wasn't working. Most people seemed unhappy. I could find little evidence that these commonly-accepted rules worked for anybody. For example: Victim mentality underpinned feigned humility. People who subscribed to the value that it's better to give than to receive often seemed unable to receive. And misfortune brought positive attention from the wider community while good luck and prosperity were rarely celebrated. I wanted to know the best way for me to live my life, so I refined the question. *What are my guiding principles?* I listed my values and my passions, which meant encountering questions like: *Were these ideas I had adopted from other people and taken as my own? How can I find out what I'm drawn towards? How can I find out what is authentic and not conditioned in me?*

As I became suspicious of directions that came from others, I began to push against the rules. I would welcome the internal consequences (my emotional and mental responses) of my actions. At least

I could learn about how I functioned and operated from my own decisions. Life became a series of test cases, learning from my actions in a conscious way. This reorientation was empowering. The more I pushed against the rules the more the potency and influence of external authority and power faded. It brought me to another conflict. My conditioned mindset was made up of rules from other people that I had adopted as my own. I saw that I believed that these rules were appropriate and valid for my life. I had absorbed and internalized a cacophony of voices telling me how I should feel, present, and behave. Some version of the outside world was inside me. These internalized rules were a greater challenge, only I now had logic and experience to validate my reasons for trusting them. The rebel in me that pushed against external rules became a spiritual rebel. Pushing against my own thought processes, beliefs, values, and comfort zones was a methodology that made sense to me if I wanted to find anything truly authentic. Breaking my own rules, testing the validity of what I had taken to be true, and being a spiritual rebel smashed my way through to clarity, love, and freedom.

A few years ago, I fractured a vertebra in my lower spine and badly damaged three discs. My own research and some medical advice suggested that three months in bed would repair my body. During that time, I was in intense pain, unable to walk or sit up without assistance for the first few weeks. Within the first day of my injuries I was exploring the spiritual insights I could gain from the experience. I had heard that when one is spiritually awake, all suffering stops. I wondered if that was true. I wasn't interested in taking pain medicine because I wanted to see if I could experience suffering. Was I suffering? There was terrible pain, yes, but was I suffering? What was the relationship between me and the pain in my body? The rebel within me doesn't accept something as true without checking it out first. I spent ten weeks in bed, but I didn't suffer. I experienced a great deal of pain, but I wasn't *suffering*.

Reorienting my attention from external influences to the internal territory of my mind, and then diving deeper into consciousness itself, is the story of how I became a spiritual rebel. The viewpoints and practices explored in this book brought me to the ongoing experience of living my life in fearless freedom.

Are you ready to be guided by your spiritual nature? When you allow your inner spiritual nature to guide your life, it shows up as a humble willingness to be open to life. You are open, vulnerable, and honest in the absence of your usual protective strategies. Your inner nature informs and modifies your personality. Let's find out what your inner nature feels, tastes, and looks like, and let's explore how you can trust it to navigate you through your life. Our goal is to have your personality serve your inner nature. This can only happen when you are committed to your own freedom; in other words, when your personality is not in charge and you are not concerned about being accepted, right, or loved. With natural confidence and humility, you respond to an impetus that is not limited by your persona and personality. When you can do this, you are in perfect alignment, fully human and fully divine, without conflict. That is freedom.

What if your belief in all of your habitual thinking processes fell away? Can you imagine how you would experience every moment if you no longer believed your thoughts? For starters you would no longer be dissatisfied, unfulfilled, and searching. If your mind's interpretation of your experience were to cease its judging, commenting, and filtering processes, what would you think and feel right now? What if all the things you have taken to be true are simply thoughts that you believe? What if you stopped looking for something better, not because you are helpless or have resigned yourself, but because you have effectively decommissioned the incessant commenting, complaining, nitpicking, reactionary, uncreative, incessantly dissatisfied mind? Your mind very seldom makes you happy, and if it does, it's a happiness that doesn't last.

In the chapters that await your attention, many self-created obstacles are dismantled for you. At other times you will have to engage in a proactive manner to break free from that which binds you. That which restricts your freedom the most, that which punishes most severely is a misused mind. Take this journey. Engage fully in the process and results will come. Keep an open mind in spite of current beliefs and trusted points of view that endeavor to resist a new paradigm.

Be honest with yourself. Are you reading this book to stimulate your intellect? Are you willing and available to let transformation happen? I didn't write this book to produce some nice inspirational quotes for you to hang on your wall. It's a journey. The chapters that follow introduce problems and provide practices that will enable you to resolve the problem. Recognizing and breaking your own rules is required. The intent is not to trade your current lifestyle with one of reckless abandon. Though this will happen for some, it is to liberate you from the limits and constraints of your personal thinking patterns and assumptions. Do not be concerned with the external evidence that might come with an internal transformation. Accept that your behavior has to change to some extent as your thinking patterns change. While your mind might call it selfishness, proceed with courage, setting aside all excuses that your mind creates. Establish right now that what you do with your life is your responsibility.

CHAPTER 2

Fearless Freedom

Freedom from something or freedom to do or be something is limited freedom because it is contingent on other circumstances. In this book we are exploring freedom itself—it is radical and beyond all constraints. Freedom itself is not a state of mind. It is rather how you experience your human nature in alignment with your spiritual nature. In my own experience fearless freedom is like a light-beam that shines when my personality is in alignment and in service to my spiritual nature. I'm at my best. There's a sense of clarity and simplicity in my body and in my mind too. If I'm distracted by a life event or feeling under pressure, I know the light is the same—it doesn't change—but my personal experience of it can modify when life is demanding.

During these times I know that my personality needs some work, support, or rest. An emotional unease creates some discomfort. There could be a new skill I need to learn or an insight I've yet to experience. I take time out. I walk the beach or dig in the earth, and I feel my natural equilibrium return. I work on the limitation that is challenging my personality. If I were to attune to the light beam and ignore the turbulence that is causing some distraction within me, I would be denying my humanity and using my spiritual nature to override what is naturally seeking resolution and further growth. There is no freedom without transparency. I don't entertain inner conflict; there is no hiding or compromise within me. I feel in a state of transparency and my spiritual nature *is* fearless freedom. As a human being I get to enjoy living with a mostly continuous sense of fearless freedom. So can you.

Fearless freedom is inside you already; it is intrinsic to your spiritual nature. It is deeper and wiser than the learned responses of your thinking processes. Take a moment right now to identify where you usually place your attention when you are not engaged with other people. Do you have the skill to ignore the stream of thoughts that flow through your mind? Can you hang out in or attune to your inner spiritual nature at will? Or do your thoughts continually demand and command your attention? Do you experience conflict between your inner spiritual place and your thoughts?

Your attention is a microphone. Where are you directing and applying amplification? Are you amplifying the stories created by your thinking mechanisms or can you amplify your inner nature where there is nothing much going on? Do you hold the opinion that your internal spiritual sense of being is boring? The truth is that your inner place, your spiritual nature is not boring; it's open, spacious and uninhibited, and your mind doesn't have the capacity to recognize these qualities. It's not here to make things exciting for you. Your mind will expect entertainment or at least an effective distraction when your attention rests within. Your spiritual nature is not concerned with any of this. It's not playing the game of *this is better than that*. It's not playing any games; it's deeper and much more expansive than your personality. It was there before your mind created its view of the world, and it will be there after your personal perspective is extinguished.

Your mind is a wonderful mechanism that creates ideas in relation to something else. For example, your mind can understand being free from something or being free to move towards something. Your mind can't understand the concept of freedom when freedom is not in relation to something else. It will dismiss freedom. The mind will associate freedom with negative concepts because the mind has to group concepts together and arrange them in order to distinguish *this* from *that*: to put this here and that there, to make this good and that bad, to name this, to categorize that, to dismiss this, to never forget that. Your mind is not capable of understanding the freedom that I'm pointing to, but your inner nature knows.

Fearless freedom is not motivated by should thoughts and ideas that validate "my" opinion. Deeper than that. True freedom is without known reference points. Freedom itself knows no fear; it is freedom for its own sake. Without familiar touchstones, how do you proceed?

There is no answer that will suffice, but proceed anyway, in spite of the cautious uncertainty of the mind. You are required to be willing to step into the unknown.

One of my students, Ellen, asked me, "What about my children if my personality takes direction from within? I feel I will stop reacting and responding. That's unfamiliar to me. My kids need a stable and consistent parent!" I replied, "What will your children do if you don't answer this call to inner authenticity, if you continue to obey the dictates of the mind, operating from fear, subject to the command of your thoughts ... How will this serve your children? The mind thinks small. It knows itself by the limitations it has learned and created. Is this the legacy you want to give your children?"

If you are beckoned by freedom itself, there is no place to hide. Prepare to expose yourself to yourself because vulnerability and falsity will be revealed. Strongly held opinions will be stripped from you. Every hiding place of the mind, no matter how noble or universal the cause, will show itself to be set in place by your limited thinking processes, complete with a personal agenda. Your mind will want to retreat in fear. It will not trust this process. Only the inner pull to freedom, the knowing that something greater is beckoning, can guide you onward. Anything else is a mind game. Faith, trust, honesty, and discernment are your best tools now. Your spiritual nature lies within you. It doesn't have a precise physical locale. It is not bound by space (or time), even though in spiritual conversation we say our spiritual nature is within us. The inward direction helps us to withdraw from life's distractions and our thoughts about our life.

When you respond to this inner beckoning, you will still function and participate in life. Trust that this is so. Those who will be drawn towards the light of your evolution will want to know what has changed for you. Some will be happy for you and others concerned. Don't be distracted by others and stay your own course. There is a real glimpse of freedom when you're not motivated by thoughts and beliefs, and are instead attuned to the rhythm of your spiritual nature, which is deeper and prior to your thinking process. When you tune in to your spiritual nature, you are in harmony with your true self. Those who are threatened by change will judge what you do and draw their conclusions quickly. Do not be concerned. You don't need approval or permission from others to take charge of your life. If it has been your habit to seek external endorsements, claim the full potency of your self-authority now and welcome the natural unfolding and maturation of your spiritual nature. Take your seat at the table–it's got your name on it. Exercise your self-authority, take charge of your spiritual path, and don't apologize for it. Step into your own power and use it. Be a spiritual rebel. Do what it takes to unearth your spiritual nature so that you can live your optimum life in fearless freedom.

There is no fear in your spiritual nature. Try out this sentence: "I don't do fear." Say it out loud right now. When you hear yourself, does it sound like bullshit? If it is bullshit, that means your mind is in charge right now, creating your moment-to-moment perceptions, limitations, and experience of reality. Your spiritual nature doesn't do fear. Can you attune to that part of you that doesn't do fear?

PRACTICE: I Don't Do Fear

Find where I don't do fear is a true statement within you. Put your hand on your belly. Why your belly? Because the sensation of touch helps to pull attention away from your thoughts, taking you out of your head and dropping attention into your torso. Slow down your breathing and relax your shoulders. Try the statement again: "I don't do fear." If it seems more plausible now, take note of what distanced you from what you felt the first time. If you have accessed your spiritual nature, then the following sentences will be true for you now. *There is no fear here. Fear doesn't happen in this place within me. My spiritual nature doesn't know what fear is.* If you don't have access to the place within you that knows nothing about fear, that means your body is holding trauma from past experiences. In this case, try to relax even more. Trauma can be in your body, that's OK. We will touch on trauma in other chapters. Your spiritual nature was around long before trauma happened to you. Practice letting go and hang out where "I don't do fear" is not an affirmation but a statement of the truth as reflected in your spiritual nature.

In this practice we removed the microphone from your thoughts and placed it at your spiritual nature. We located your spiritual nature by identifying one of its qualities–fearlessness. In the case of unreleased trauma held in the body, your microphone will amplify your body's learned experience of fear instead of dropping deeper into your spiritual nature. Whatever your experience, don't judge it. We are mapping the territory that you have to walk in order for you to live in fearless freedom.

CHAPTER 3

Courage

Are you reading this book in the hope that the words alone are enough to change your life? I hope not, because it would be a pity if you were to join ranks with the many spiritual aspirants who are well-read and meditate regularly, yet have no interest in getting down and dirty with their beliefs and thinking habits. A spiritual lifestyle alone doesn't lead to freedom; an internal and personal shakeup is necessary. You will need courage if you want to be a spiritual rebel and live your life in fearless freedom. Change has to happen.

You will need courage to do things differently. You will need courage to live outside your comfort zone. Your call to action is to go against the ideas you hold about yourself. Consider the example of a client of mine. We'll call him "Bob." Bob knows his marriage is over. In many ways he has already left it, and yet he hasn't shared this with his wife. They continue in marriage therapy because he wants to make fully sure that his wife has every opportunity to grow from her exposure to the therapeutic process. He believes he is being kind, giving her a chance to work on herself and her ability to be in relationship. In truth he's being dishonest with himself, his wife, and his therapist. Why? Because he believes that to initiate conflict or pain is always a bad course of action.

Bob was a peacemaker in his volatile family of origin, and he continues to recreate calmness even though he knows he has mentally and emotionally already left the marriage. *I'm waiting for the right time,* he says to himself. There is no right time to break up his marriage— that's not what peacemakers do. There is no right time to break a golden rule (e.g. peace at all costs) that was put in place during childhood. Golden rules help children to survive and in adulthood we unconsciously believe that maintaining the same habits of behavior will keep us safe. Bob needs courage to have a willingness to see what conditioned responses are motivating his thoughts and actions. He needs courage to step out of his comfort zone and take an authentic course of action.

Like Bob, there is nothing you can't face. It is your thoughts that try to convince you otherwise. Your mind can't give you an accurate gauge of the stakes involved because its agenda is to preserve belief systems that protect the habitual belief that is your personal identity. Loosen your investment in beliefs that bind you to your habitual and contracted viewing point. Stop waiting for your life to be easy. Stop hoping for someone or something to save you. You can do this. You can develop courage to choose unfamiliar options.

Courage shows up in the ability to challenge your own belief system. Courage is present when you can honestly challenge your perception of the world as you have set it up in your mind. Courage is an ability to take action in spite of anxiety or fear. The word courage has its root in the French word Coeur that translates as "heart." I'm not sure if courage comes from the heart, but I know it doesn't come from the mind. Courage doesn't originate from a believed idea.

In Bob's case he has no familiarity with how to initiate the painful transition of separation from his wife. As he recognizes the limiting belief, *I am a peacemaker*, he feels an opening that comes with a fresh insight into his thinking patterns. Next, he remembers and understands where his role of peacemaker originated. It can be a learned habit from observing the same behavior in a parent or guardian, or it can be a role we developed in order to protect ourselves. With these steps: (a) recognizing the belief (b) identifying how it was created, and (c) deciding to no longer support the belief, we can establish a distance from the thought pattern. With this distance established, the belief begins to break away from you—like an iceberg drifting off into the ocean.

Sometimes we recognize the belief and, when we identify how this belief was created, we might feel emotional pain as memories emerge. What makes beliefs stubborn and resistant to change is unresolved trauma held in our bodies. For change to happen in these difficult cases, you will need to face the inner pain by exploring and revisiting your past so that you can heal and free your body from trauma. Beliefs (which inform patterns of behavior) that came with trauma were hard earned because your mind associates and credits your beliefs with what kept you safe. Having a strong attachment to beliefs is natural. And these beliefs aren't wholly wrong. Maybe these beliefs did keep you safe, but chances are you don't need them anymore. We can't surrender a belief until we heal and resolve the original wounds associated with its creation. There is no quick fix around this process.

Try not to deny a persistent and recurring belief as mere thought when, in spite of being recognized, it still retains the potency to influence how you feel. There is no courage in such avoidance. If a belief keeps resurfacing even though you know it's merely a thought, then you have something to unpack, something to learn about the original experience that first created the thinking pattern. This takes a lot of courage. Place your attention on that courage and embrace unfamiliar action in spite of your mind's best efforts to concoct a narrative about your safety. See how your mind can offer a sufferable, comforting familiarity in its best efforts to help you survive. There is no freedom in playing survival games with your mind long after the threat is gone.

Reserve the experience of fear for the very rare occasions in which you are in physical danger and honor those feelings as essential to your survival in those rare cases. As you step into unknown territory try not to draw on emotions, practice engaging curiosity instead. Curiosity is open to the unknown. It doesn't create fantasy or project an outcome. It is present to what is happening right now. Stay in the wonderment about what might happen next. It's innocent and available to you. It widens your capacity to experience beyond your familiar template. Proceed with determination and break the rules of your own making. Be curious about the outcomes.

Not conforming to your own rules, stepping into the unknown, can trigger fear, but only if you have established that thought-to-emotion thinking habit. If you are not in objective danger, there is no need to entertain fear—ever. Breaking out of your habitual thinking pattern is dangerous only for the idea of you (which your mind has created). In practical terms you are not in immediate danger, otherwise you wouldn't be sitting down to read this book. Blessings begin when you step out of your comfort zone. In the end, one only regrets the chances that one didn't take.

PRACTICE: I'd Never Do That

List three actions that go against your idea of who you think you are. Be both practical and sensible in your selection. Be sure to identify things that don't involve breaking the law or being malicious towards others. Choose one item from your list and try it. Your task is to practically cultivate courage. Don't engage memories of emotions such as fear, shame, or lack. You don't need to add to an emotional memory bank. Stay present and take action from a place of courage. Do at least one thing from your list of three that you thought you would or could never do.

During one of my intense eras of introspection, I remember taking a lift home from a meditation gathering on the back of a motorcycle from a man who was the antithesis of whom I would be attracted to. My kind of guy would stand in the background and is understated; mystery interests me. This biker was all about his self-image and the conquest of the next fresh face in town. En route home, he pulled into a bar. I had a cup of tea. I felt uneasy and went to the ladies' bathroom, looked in the mirror, and started talking to my reflection. *What's going on here?* I had an unfamiliar internal feeling that I had to explore. *He's everything I judge and dislike in men.* My innate wisdom replied, *You've got to drop these judgments.* To which my thoughts replied, *Hmmm, I don't think highly of women who play this game either...and that's another bundle of judgments.* I looked straight at my image in the mirror and said to myself, "You think you're above all of this don't you? You think you know better, because you can see through the games he plays in order to get laid." Insight finally arrived, *I'm the one caught in games of power and superiority. This guy is being himself, doing what he does. I'm the one caught up in my head.* At this, I decided that it was time to shatter my conditioned belief that worked until now which stated that

I'd never be with a guy like that. I walked back to the bar and said, "Would you like us to get a room?"

The exercise worked. It cut straight through my own bullshit. For the next two weeks I hung out with him, and I had a great time. I knew that I had to break through my projections where I imagined others were judging me for being with him. I knew that I was projecting my own judgments onto him as well as onto myself. Pushing through brought me to the place where I could laugh at my own drama and disclose my charade to the unassuming biker. He then shared that my read on his motivation was accurate. He had a sex addiction that he battled with for over 30 years. He thought he disguised it well. Undoubtedly, I sensed a sexual agenda that I wasn't comfortable with. Unable to remain objective, my personality created a position of arrogant superiority for me, dismissing what was going on for him and making it all about me. We laughed when we recognized that we used each other, albeit for very different reasons.

What rules of behavior limit your living? Are there fears, anxieties, compulsions, or addictions that influence your thoughts and actions? You can cower in front of the obstacles you associate with your *I would never do that* list, or you can walk straight through them. But you have to first know what the obstacles are. Then consider your actions with care. You need to know what you are doing and why. Admit to yourself where you seek personal recognition, acceptance, love, or familiarity through your behavior. There is no courage in subtle manipulation. These and all limitations exist only in your mind. When a situation arises and it's something you would never do, or not want to be seen doing, then do it!

CHAPTER 4

On Not Playing Safe

When I was on my spiritual path, I was drawn to service. I am still in service—it makes sense to me to be of use to others, but I had to first clean up why and when I would serve, and find courage to do so. As a spiritual seeker I spent time in India, where I had many opportunities to help others. On a few occasions I stayed in an ashram that was dedicated to service. On my first stay I felt right at home working from before dawn until evening.

A year later I revisited this ashram and had planned to stay for several weeks. On my first day I recognized that my service was giving me a role to play, something to do, an ability to be of use to others, and here's the crunch: that was a *good thing* in my seeker value system.

Am I in service because my mind says it's the right thing to do, or is my spiritual nature directing my actions? I had to answer this question and discern my motivations. I decided to refuse to be of help in an environment where service was obligatory, to see what that might trigger for me. I had to find courage to push against the indisputable, high value of service that was both in me and in the ashram. I had to give myself the experience that had never been entertained before now; I had to refuse to help others in a place that was dedicated to service. For five very uncomfortable days I resisted my personality trait and allowed every emotion and judgment arise and pass by without having any of that internal drama influence my resolve. What happened? The exercise freed up more access to my spiritual nature.

After five days I could easily discern when I was driven towards action by the dictates of my conditioned mind (*I should…*, *I can so I will…*, *It's good to be of service…*, *It's expected…*), and I could now easily ignore these directives. I learned to recognize when there was an urge that stirred from deeper within me. The inner urge seemed to be in harmony with a greater order that usually made sense to me later. I had become familiar with not having a rational reason, in the moment, to support why I was serving or not, and I learned to trust the process. That's what requires courage: following through regardless of habits and expectations you have about yourself or from others. The right thing, or the safe thing, according to your mind can be the opposite of the urge from your spiritual nature. When you stop obeying your mind the volume of your mental narrative decreases. Switch the microphone to your spiritual nature and break your habits. Have the courage to make the shift.

My experience now, some fifteen years later, is that my mind and my personality are tools that help me function practically in the world. Like any tool I pick them up when needed, and I set them down afterwards. Fearless freedom is the constant underlying experience. I have an expansive view of life from my broad vantage point. The "Jac" story, how this woman thinks and acts, features as an ongoing show on a small television set to the side of the wide, perhaps infinite scenery. She is held and supported within my spiritual nature like the small TV has its place within the vastness. When I come to an opportunity for personal growth my story increases in volume. I work on myself and learn something new about my human experience. To engage in a personal story and view Jac's world as if it were all that exists would require a denial of my spiritual nature. When something needs processing, it doesn't take over. That's way too much drama, and I know better than to let my mind be the only show in town. I'm not the center of my universe. It is more authentic to state that my spiritual nature contains the universe and Jac is a very small part of that universe.

When you believe yourself to be your personality, and you know better than that, you compromise yourself. When you inquire within and get honest with yourself, you probably find that you are like most people: frequently defending the person you think you are, concerned about how others perceive you, and micromanaging your own behaviors in order to control your image. By doing these things, you've allowed yourself to be controlled by the relatively shallow forces of your social milieu and have opted out of standing uncompromisingly in your own power. You think you've made an easy choice, but in fact you've chosen a prison. Admittedly you don't have to stick your neck out much in this prison, but you'll forever be required to follow other people's rules, to plead for their acceptance, to ask for their permission, to beg for their endorsement. Try not to be at the bidding of uncomfortable feelings. Feelings come and go, and opinions do, too. Don't be swayed towards action by emotional reactions.

Whether it is conscious or unconscious at this point, you know you are not who your mind thinks you are. When we become aware that we are not defined by our thoughts, beliefs, or personality, we have to be honest with ourselves at the risk of not playing nice. We must stop defending and protecting the personal "me." Life itself is endeavoring to strip away our inauthenticities and that's the spiritual path.

Why would you defend what is not you? In one directive sentence: stop taking things personally. Instead be quiet. Watch what your emotions are up to. Notice your judging thoughts and let these things pass by. Don't act out from personal reactions. It creates drama and conflict within you. Conflict with others is not nearly as toxic as the internal conflict it creates in you. Please stop doing that to yourself. How? Don't take anything personally. Taking things personally is a learned habit. It's safer to remain in the familiar position of upholding hard-earned beliefs and habits that create your "me" story than to step into a territory that is unknown and uncontrollable by your mind. It is fear that makes you think comments, actions, and events are about you. Don't trade your beautiful spiritual nature to uphold the character you play. Habits like spending energy defending it, recreating new personal stories, further alienating that character from the open invitation to go home to your spiritual nature must be set aside now. Every thought, opinion, and judgment that you defend serves to protect and sustain the personal character—the one that your mind thinks you are. Have the courage to recognize these defensive habits that were adopted in ignorance.

Stop playing small even if you think everyone else behaves like this, too. This way of approaching life is almost universal. It's a shared experience and a persistent habit that sticks like glue, binding people together, endlessly defending and judging each other. The only way to resolve these behavioral patterns is to get out of them.

Subjective personal thought creates the global shared reality of inauthenticity and pretense. See your part in the universal habit with objectivity, not with judgment nor emotion. Take a chance, let your world destabilize a little. Let go of your assumptions about yourself and about reality. Break the habit of reacting from adopted perspectives; there is no freedom in that. Protecting, defending, hiding—these are learned habits that hold fear in place. When a not so pleasant aspect of your personality shows up, celebrate the exposure and let the personality reshape itself to a softer version of itself. There's strength in this kind of softness. Celebrate when you get to see a personality blindspot—you are breaking free from ignorance. There is no need to hide, ignore or lie about your personal character. Be done with such self-deception!

CHAPTER 5

It's Not You; It's Your Brain

From the moment we are born, our senses collect impressions that are converted into electro-chemical signals in the brain. Every thought, every idea has a corresponding electrical neural signal. A repeated thought reactivates a route or pathway already established. When we recognize a thought it's the consequence of a signal firing along the same neural pathway as before. The brain creates a network of these pathways by drawing together loosely connected associations, grouping concepts together and attributing meaning to them. A network becomes reinforced and strengthened through repetitive usage. Over time, as we habitually entertain the same thoughts, the brain sets up a default network which can be quite resistant to change. The more we repeat, the stronger the network gets. This is why mental habits and beliefs are hard to break.

The brain networks have a primary function to recognize and repeat, whether that familiar/habitual behavior is healthy for us or not. When we repeat and avoid creating new neural pathways there is temporary ease and safety in the familiar because our brain kicks back into autopilot using learned patterns from the past to give us an experience in the present. At these times we are experiencing from our previously built database (memory), and we are not in the present moment. See if you notice that the comfort of familiarity is absent when we are learning something new. It's important to let yourself enjoy being inspired, creative, having new experiences because firing new neural pathways is what keeps the brain active and dynamic.

One neural network, an intricately linked structure, is called the *Default Mode Network* (DMN). It's also referred to as the self-referencing network. Its primary task is to establish a sense of self, a personal self, and in doing so maintain stability so that we can function well on a practical level. As the generating system for the self, the DMN supplies drive and reward so that we can get things done. It is where self-reflection takes place as well as narrative memory with thoughts about the past and the future. Its job is to create and repeat a familiar sense of "me."

In the absence of some skill and understanding about our minds, the DMN can draw together data from experiences that have nothing to do with us using it to recreate and reinforce the sense of self. Taking things personally, making things relevant to me when they don't have to be, thinking about whether my actions and words will bring acceptance or rejection—all of these thoughts are products of the self-referencing DMN overstretching its reach. If we are not managing our thoughts, the DMN will continue to build personal identity through filtering benign information that is gleaned from our senses and making most everything about "me." Left unmanaged it creates thinking habits that maintain consistency in the stories we tell ourselves about ourselves.

Consider the example of my friend, Angela. One morning I dropped by Angela's home for tea and conversation. As she opened the door with an immediate, "You won't believe what I found!", it was clear she was having an emotional reaction to something. I asked what had happened. "Look at what I discovered under Tom's side of our mattress," as she slapped a porn magazine in front of me. "We've been married for two years. Why is he buying this crap? Did I marry a man who has the emotional intelligence of a sixteen-year-old?" I replied, "Angela, this isn't about you." She couldn't hear me. "How can he support an industry where women are exploited?" Again, "Angela, this isn't about you." "I thought we had a great sex life, but clearly he doesn't think so." "Angela, this has nothing to do with you, nor your sex life." She stopped. "Oh! You've said that a few times. I hear you now." She became calm and dropped out of her dramatic personal response and began to perceive things differently. She saw that Tom was managing his sexual needs in a safe and personal way that fit within the bounds of their marriage. She knew that they needed to communicate more and cultivate a deeper intimacy in their relationship, allowing spaces for their differences so they could explore new ways to support each other's needs.

When Angela first saw the magazine, her DMN filtered the benign data: *my partner enjoys soft porn.* Her self-referencing capacity was activated. She lost all objectivity and created stories about her relationship that she believed to be true. Some weeks later, she told me that she and Tom had a good laugh at her reaction. She had felt threatened and needed to work on her own confidence within the relationship. The DMN will make associations and find personal resonance with ordinary events that have nothing to do with us in its effort to generate and protect a sense of personal identity.

When you process perception through your DMN, you will naturally shy away from what is already not known because the unknown is unstable. In an effort to maintain stable, familiar ground, the DMN will interpret data from experiences outside of its frame of reference as fearful, and it can stimulate anxiety to support its agenda. These emotions are a natural repellant away from what is new and unfamiliar, even though what is unknown can be rich in opportunities for your growth. Your DMN will always encourage you to fall back to what is known.

As we move towards spiritual freedom, we need to embrace what is unknown. We must learn how to perceive and communicate without filtering data through our DMNs. Begin by paying close attention to the thoughts about you that go through your mind as you perform a task. For example, when you do an act of kindness, do you make a point of having it noticed? As you cook a meal for friends do you consider their possible approval or disapproval of you via the meal (which is different than cooking solely for the pleasure of all)? Do you modify how you hold your body so that you will look younger or thinner? Are you disingenuous when you have sex in order to influence your lover to approve of you or want you more? What actions come with a hidden personal agenda? These patterns of thought are driven by your DMN. It makes everything about "you."

PRACTICE: Identify Personal Agendas and Drop Them

You are equipped with the ability to participate in life without making actions and interactions about you. Pay attention to the internal narrative that influences what you do and what you say. Identify personal agendas and drop them. They can be manipulative, and you'll notice many that you'd rather not admit to yourself. Don't take this work personally. The task is to rewire your brain so that your speech and actions can happen independently to the me who would like to benefit from them. Things are rarely about you. Let this truth shine through. There is relief in this recognition.

PART 2

IT'S ALL IN THE MIND

CHAPTER 6

With and Without the DMN

On my journey toward freedom, I dedicated several years to full time engagement in spiritual practices. I was committed to being aware of my mind in every moment. I watched and observed my thoughts objectively. I was drawn to be in silence as much as was practicable, and I spent many hours every day in meditation. I was living in India, and my lifestyle was simple. Whatever physical activity I did, I did so consciously, observing all without comment. If my mind prompted an action that had a personal agenda, I would not support it and waited until something deeper than personal thought would stimulate action.

The following account is an experience where my DMN turned off, burned out, and stopped working. I had no awareness of what the DMN was at the time, though there was an intuitive recognition that changes in the brain are inevitable with spiritual awakening. At times, my spiritual journey involved extreme measures. My intention here is to offer a more moderate route to attain the same results. An awareness of the DMN, its role, and how it functions is central to understanding how the brain changes with spiritual awakening.

One morning, I was in the shower, and I felt a sensation on the left side of my head. It felt like there were parts of my brain pulling away from each other. I put my hand to my head and supported myself against a wall with my other hand. The sensations felt as though structures were breaking down inside my brain. I had a thought that kept fear at bay: *I'm either going mad or this has something to do with my spiritual work. If it's madness and I'm to be admitted to a psychiatric hospital here in India, then so be it. I'll learn something from that experience, too.* And I stopped resisting. I don't remember what else happened that day, though I suspect my daily routine of silence and meditation prevailed.

The following morning when I awoke my hand stretched out to my bedside table and picked up my passport. I read the name and date of birth (my name and birthdate) and looked at the image. I got out of bed and walked to a mirror. I read the name on the passport aloud and looked at the photo and back to my face…the photo…my face until my brain registered recognition. Next, I went to a calendar hanging in the kitchen, and my eyes fell on a date where all the earlier ones were crossed out. I would look at the date, day of the week, month, and year until another recognition activated a sense of time. Third step was to look at my date of birth and today's date, and I would slowly work out what age I was. This became my morning routine for some months. A period of two years with no thoughts had begun. Nighttime dreams ceased also. There was stillness, silence, nothing going on. I didn't have the thought that my mind was quiet. I could neither like nor dislike my experience because I didn't have access to concepts to compare, evaluate, or create an opinion about anything. My DMN stopped working, and I assume, based on the sensations I felt in my head, that it burned itself out.

All of a sudden a large selection of basic English words sounded foreign to me. When I bought food, I had no idea what my local shop-keeper was saying to me. Perhaps I smiled back at him, perhaps I looked bewildered. I'm not sure. I walked into a bookstore and bought an English dictionary. When I heard a word that sounded strange, I would look up its meaning. I was relearning some vocabulary. Words that lost their meaning included "candle," "soup," "hinge," "library," and "fuel." I didn't plan to place my passport within arm's reach of my bed or mark off days in the kitchen calendar as they passed. I didn't decide to purchase a dictionary, or that looking up unfamiliar words would help restore my vocabulary. An innate functionality was guiding my way.

I was living in the present moment, responding (at least enough to not cause undue concern to others) to what life presented. Each morning my actions would recreate a timeline and my place within it. Identifying as "Jac" was no longer an automatic process. Daily re-recognition of a woman, her name, established my impersonal viewpoint through her eyes. Within a couple of months, viewing the passport photo triggered a sustaining association between my body and the image. I no longer needed to take the steps to a mirror or the calendar. My routine during those years included a phone call to my parents every couple of weeks. I'm not sure if the frequency of my calls changed, though I know what I said did. I made calls from a public phone box, on a street. I would look around me and describe what I was seeing. There was nothing to say about "me," so I would speak about what I saw in that moment. My siblings told me that I seemed withdrawn, disconnected from the world, that my personality changed. One of my sisters told me that she felt as though I had died, that she had lost her sister. I had no response.

In addition to the absence of any personal experience, I lost the ability to empathize with other people. The experience of another struck me as theirs and theirs alone, and because I had no capacity to register my own experiences as personal, there was no way to meet them on a personal level. Life's circumstances, however, eventually brought me back to my own culture. Thoughts began to flow again, and I made an effort to relearn how to generate conversation and empathize. Five years after my DMN burn out experience I was sitting with a new friend and wondered to myself: *What do people talk about? I know how to look around me and talk about what I see—I can do that. Is that the art of conversation?* I could think and peruse, imagine and evaluate, but I couldn't as yet talk about "me." I had yet to relearn the skill of presenting a personal perspective.

That experience and phase of my life was significant in the spiritual awakening process. Now, again there are thoughts that sometimes cruise through my mind, and sometimes there is an ongoing flow. I have nighttime dreams and random thoughts, and I participate in life with a spectrum of emotions. The main difference between before that experience and now is that I recognize my thoughts primarily as thoughts, and their story content is secondary. There is ongoing distance from thinking. Thoughts are not readily believed and are never fully believed. I don't seem to be able to believe thoughts in the way I used to.

Implicit in all thinking is the creation of the idea of separation, it is essential for effective functioning. We need a sense of self and dualistic language so that we can participate in life. My attention doesn't seem to lock into the personal viewpoint. To say that another way, the personal doesn't seem to be able to absorb all of my attention. The volume of my mental chatter is low. The personal "me" shows up within a broader, expansive context. Even if the contracted viewpoint of the personal "me" were to return again, even though I remember it can at times be a hellish way to live, I am open to that experience as well. I am not able to generate resistance to that, or any, possibility.

CHAPTER 7

The Need to be Right

The primary purpose of the Default Mode Network is to generate a sense of self and to ensure its continuity and survival. It gathers your beliefs, values, and impressions of your social environment, work, family, friends, and self-image, and it draws them together to create a stable reference point that you recognize as yourself within a life. It sets up and maintains an identity. It is who you think you are and thus a mistaken identity. The personal self that is a construct of your DMN is not you. If you explore your personal identity, created and supported by neural circuitry, you will not find substance deeper than thought.

To live in obedience to the limitations of a brain-made sense of who you are causes suffering. And it is exhausting to continually reinforce the thought of "me," as though your life depends on it. And that's literally what's at stake for the DMN. There is no rest to be had when we are responding to an insatiable survival agenda to protect what's essentially an idea. To follow its commands is hypnosis. You have the capacity to observe the DMN thought flow. Believing it to be true, that you are the "me" idea, is the absence of freedom.

What if you were to go against the definition of "you," as created by your neural pathways? Step away from the stable model of (mistaken) identity that your brain has created for you. Going against the definition of "you" that you hold (as supported by the DMN) means breaking your own rules. For example when there is a conflict of opinions and you assert your opinion over someone else's, this connects with how your brain defines you as a person. Until you get some distance from these mechanisms you will not want to go against who you are as a person. It feels threatening. Your thinking processes will avoid the possibility that you could be wrong. It feels uncomfortable to admit you are wrong and back down when your opinion is equated with your identity. If you feel the need to be right, it's because the "me" identity depends on it. As long as your thinking process refers to your DMN, you will defend yourself and if your opinion is proven incorrect, your sense of yourself and your self-confidence will be undermined. You can feel deflated, misunderstood, and disrespected. Self-preservation draws us towards people who agree with our opinion: people who support us, empathize with us, and make us feel good about ourselves. We are safe again and we relax.

Experiences that challenge us personally are painful. Yet they come with a gift—they weaken mistaken identity by placing a wedge in the brain-made sense of self. Welcome discomfort. It's an opportunity to see how invested we have become in the personal self-identity.

PRACTICE: Choose Wisely

You can break the habit of being who you think you are. For the next twenty-four hours, don't say anything that reinforces your personal identity. Don't automatically follow through on your habitual regular routine and see what comes up for you. See that the familiarity of speech and routine is a trick of mind that keeps repeated thinking processes in charge. This is an opportunity to break the connection between habitual self-defending, self-sustaining thoughts and your actions. It's important that you know how this feels as it plays out in you—you need to get familiar with the feeling and let it become the new normal. As a practice it launches you well on your way to being fully conscious in every moment.

The self-preservation component in your subjective perception will work to rebuild your sense of self; it cannot see through its own mechanisms. We can't get an objective perspective on the mechanics as long as we believe we are the identity it preserves. When you know that your brain has created *the story of you*, relief comes. There is expansion, and you can view the separate personal story from a wider view, from a distance.

PRACTICE: Do Something Wrong, Don't Do What's Right

List ten personal beliefs exploring your understanding of "right" and "wrong." Each sentence should begin with either "It's right to…" or "It's wrong to…" List a total of ten. Search for examples of what you believe are absolute rules. Set about breaking each of your ten beliefs. Use common sense and don't break the laws of the land, even if you come to see them with a great deal of distance. If "it's wrong to break the law" is one of your beliefs, then be wise and let your action cause no harm to yourself or others!

People who are very self-conscious and critical about their bodies have found that spending a few days on a nudist beach broke some personal laws. Another said that asking their boss for a raise, for no reason, broke an absolute. Each person has their own list of behaviors that are off limits. Give yourself the experience of stepping outside your definition of yourself and enjoy doing it!

Doing the opposite of a value upheld by your personal identity will force you to create new neural networks. Your reliance on your DMN will weaken. There are many small steps you can take that might not be noticed by anyone until the accumulated effect shines from you in an open availability to life. The potent strides are when you break personal rules and beliefs that you might be embarrassed to admit, even to yourself. Do not associate unfamiliar activity with lack of safety (which leads to fear); we are not trying to fit new experiences into the judgmental framework of safe or unsafe, right or wrong. We are breaking your loyalty to the false identity you hold of yourself by going against some of its defining beliefs and dropping attachments to being right.

CHAPTER 8

Task Oriented Network

Without a functioning DMN, I was able to cycle a bicycle and cook meals. I could complete basic tasks that required my attention during a regular day. I can't speak to the quality of my participation, just that I continued to function and take care of daily life.

We can imagine that without the sense of "me" that life will fall apart—it's not true. Why? Because another part of your brain, a different neural network, manages planning, action, and executing tasks. Neuroscience has identified what part of the brain enables us to get stuff done. When it was first identified, this neural network was called the *Task Positive Network*, and, more recently, it's referred to as the *Task Oriented Network* (TON). Same thing—two names.

When you put your attention on a task your TON fires signals that enable you to do what you need to do. If you make the task personal, if you have an agenda that involves a "me" story then you are engaging the DMN at the same time. Herein lies the problem. When we use both circuits together, we are less efficient and distracted from the task at hand because we are accommodating another motivation that has influence on what we do and how we do it. Take the personal out of it, or, to rephrase that directive, stop running your DMN when your TON is the appropriate tool for the job.

The mind can imagine that if the personal me isn't around to make life run smoothly then everything will fall apart. That's not true at all. The DMN has an inflated sense of its own importance. It can't imagine its own absence. It runs the belief that nothing happens without its input. Its task is to generate the sense of self and so it tries to make itself indispensable in its efforts to create a sense of self. It is literally self-perpetuating. Do you believe your DMN? Do you think that without "you" in charge that your life would fall into disarray? Your TON is what gets stuff done.

PRACTICE: Disentangle your DMN from your TON

Stop running personal "me" thoughts when you are doing stuff. For example, when at work don't try to get attention for staying late. At home, cook a meal without looking for praise. Don't entertain a personal agenda when you perform tasks. Keep it clean. Get stuff done without making it about you.

At this point I would like to remind you that the fields of science and spirituality are only beginning to explore common ground. It's early days in their relationship. Neuroscience has not explored (and perhaps not considered) the subtle workings of the DMN that overlap the self-generating agenda with the TON. There is a lot of scope for collaboration between science and spirituality in the future.

CHAPTER 9

Perception

Both your brain and your mind are tools for you to use. Your brain is a product of evolution with the primary purpose of guiding adaptive behavior for your safety. It is the mechanical system that designs and supports how you experience. Your mind is your thoughts together with your awareness of your thoughts. You have thoughts; you are not your thoughts. You have a brain; you are not your brain. You have a sense of a personal self; you are not your personal self.

The personal as we have discussed is created by the DMN. This network straddles both sides of the brain with minor dominance on the left side. Science has identified physical regions of the brain as lobes and assigns functions to these lobes individually and co-operatively. Yet the DMN crisscrosses several lobes, drawing together what it needs to enable a personal perspective for functioning.

In spirituality we talk about an impersonal lens of perception. We use the impersonal when we don't make things about us, that is, when we don't take things personally. Is the impersonal viewpoint a different neural network? We don't know. If it's not another network, could an impersonal viewpoint be our experience of a healthier usage of the DMN? Impersonally, we have a sense of self and we perceive objectively, without reference to a "me" story. My personal experiences influence me to think that the DMN is central to the impersonal viewpoint, and that the difference between poor and proper usage of the DMN lies in whether we believe that the self that it generates is who we are. Do you identify with the personal self or not?

The DMN offers a sense of self. That self is an essential component in intimate friendships and personal depth. It helps us to know what it means to be human. Without a DMN we are not bothered by anything at all and that can suffice in some lifestyles. My destiny was to return to my own culture where life situations highlighted skills that I needed to relearn. As mentioned earlier, I was naturally drawn to relearning how to participate in casual conversation.

Listing some defining features of the personal and the impersonal lenses of perception helps define their differences. By objectifying and identifying both, we can get more distance and recognize them as tools we can choose to pick up and set down. For spiritual freedom we need to be clear around how we use our brain to view and participate in life. We don't have enough neuroscientific findings as yet to give clear pointers on how to use our brains for specific results. And so you have to feel into this sample material for yourself and have some *ah ha* moments as you deepen your own understanding of how your brain works for you.

Personal Perspective Tenets

- I believe what I think about me and I am who I think I am.

- I am separate from you and I see more differences than similarities between us.

- My sense of self worth comes from how others see me.

- I compare myself to others and my findings tell me how I am doing.

- I don't love myself and I need others' love to prove to me that I may be lovable.

- My need for others to love me is greater than my desire to love myself.

- My emotions are close to the surface and can include anxiety, self-doubt, fear, self-consciousness…

Impersonal Perspective Tenets

- I have a sense of individuality, it is held within a wider view of what I perceive.

- Everything is connected to each other at a more fundamental level than how it looks.

- I know that I am both lovable and capable. I don't need to prove either.

- Trust is my default. I'm suspicious and cautious only when given good reason to be.

- Facts are subjective perceptions. Useful but I'm not tied to them.

The personal perspective creates suffering by creating a personal one who can suffer. As you set your sights on fearless freedom, work on becoming familiar with the impersonal perspective. The impersonal will become the default lens and the habit of viewing personally will fade away. In my work I have found two primary contributors that activate and sustain the personal perspective.

The first is trauma, and the second is language. We know that trauma is the underlying cause that makes "me" stories painful. Add trauma to a sense of self and our survival mechanism will reinterpret the sense of self to be who we are. For example, we can say "I have a body." Add trauma to that body, and our brain converts "I have a body" into "I am my body." The wider view becomes narrow and personalized. Intensity increases the stakes and we focus on self-preservation. When our identity is compromised and mistaken, we will suffer because it's fundamentally not true. This is why resolving trauma is a necessary part of maintaining a sustained awakening.

Our language center begins to develop in early childhood, when we comprehend that objects have names. As we learn how to communicate effectively, we are taught how to label things, people, experiences, emotions, and the like. A fundamental separation between yourself and others, you and life, was erroneously assumed as fact. Through language each of us became a subject that perceives and experiences objects. Language helps us interpret the world in story. We tell ourselves stories all the time. The categorizing of information in terms of opposites: do or don't, win or lose, good or bad, like or dislike, and so on. These dichotomies lend themselves to value judgments.

Every belief, every value, is another story. See that language is a tool. Pick it up and set it down. It's an interpretation of the world, of you, of life. It's limited and inaccurate.

PRACTICE: Where Am I Looking from?

Ask yourself where you are looking from right now. Get familiar with recognizing when you are running a personal "me" story or if you are in the more spacious impersonal landscape. I would like you to check in to see where you are looking from every half an hour for the next five years! It's that important an exercise because every time you check in you are becoming a little more aware and a little less caught in the content of your thoughts. You will naturally become more present, relaxed, and open to life.

CHAPTER 10

Time and Space Filter

The concepts of time and space together create a filter that supports our ability to perceive the world around us. It is made of two parts, and when they function together, they create an important filter that stabilizes and contextualizes our perceptual experience. Time and space are not part of the personal or impersonal viewpoints. They are a filter lens that is in place before we engage either the impersonal or the personal. Time and space are the supporting environment, the solid surface of the table where we can pick up and set down the personal and impersonal tools of perception. Perhaps you have had experiences of time stopping, time distorting, time travel, or the absence of time. I like to think that premonitions are kinks in the timeline, places where a scene from the future shows up momentarily before its due date. People who meditate often report that time in meditation can skip by unusually quickly. In contrast, meditation sessions during which the personal story making mechanism is on high volume make the practice go very slowly. Our perception of time is ambiguous and personal because it's created by our perceiving mechanisms.

Many years ago, I attended a series of meditation with relaxation workshops. It was a wonderful experience to lay on the floor and be swept away to a depth within myself, where I could totally let go and trust the tutor to bring me back to the here and now. Quite often I wouldn't be able to speak or go for refreshments with the group afterwards. These sessions encouraged me to withdraw from my sense of "self" to the extent that socialization felt jarring to my deeply relaxed nervous system. At the end of one guided meditation I was lying on the floor and opened my eyes. People around me were gathering their gear and preparing to leave. Without any thought I heard my mind say *stop* and the scene in the room, of which I was part, froze. My mind said *go back*, and what I had just perceived slowly rewound at the same speed as it happened a moment before. It was like an old VCR tape rewinding and you can see the images going in reverse. *Stop,* and it froze again. *Go,* and the very same scenes continued as they did before. People did the same movements I saw a moment before, as if for the first time. They moved once but for me a replay was possible. I continued to play with the commands of going forward, going backwards, and freeze-framing what was happening for several minutes. I recognized that the room was almost empty in some frames and this meant something to the personal "me." Then my first conscious personal thought came: *Oh I'm disturbing the timeline.* Because I believed my own thought I was pulled from outside of time to within time, where I was an individual attending a spiritual gathering on a Tuesday evening. Back into my own movie again, subject to time and space, my body, and my thoughts. Of course, nobody was aware of my experience, and the timeline is untouchable because time is not a thing independent of our perception of it. We create it and by adopting the concept of it, it becomes real. We can't touch it, taste it. It remains a concept. And yet we respond to the concept of time and can feel imprisoned by it. We imagine we don't have enough time, and most of us believe that having more of it is a good thing. Just as we create our experience of "me," we also create our experience of time.

What I learned from that experience stayed with me. I learned that space and time are quite separate, that time is the first to deconstruct when we are doing spiritual work. Space remains as the structure of time loosens. Space is more fundamental to the building blocks of our reality; it's prior to time. As we orient inwardly the independence of space from the timeline is significant. We can't have time without space already in view.

PART 3

GETTING INTO IT

CHAPTER 11

Non-Duality with a Twist

Have you recognized that you have a capacity that is looking through the space-time filter, the impersonal and personal lenses of perception? If you do, then who or what is it that is looking? You can't be the object of your perception. You are not the story you tell yourself about yourself, because you have the ability to view that personal self from a much wider viewpoint. What is it that views the mechanism that creates who you can sometimes think you are? Are you that viewing mechanism? Do you need to be something or someone at all? Can you roll with this line of questioning and not replace the personal, separate self with what amounts to a more sophisticated identity? Try to get familiar with having no reference point, no landing place. If you can sense or intuit where "I" am looking from right now, you will see that all story content is at a distance from where viewing comes from. The viewing itself has no content. The verb or action of viewing takes place without a viewer doing the viewing and without any content that can be viewed. Prior to diversity, without parts, there is only viewing. We can exchange the word "view" to "perceive" and state that the verb or action of perceiving takes place without a perceiver doing the perceiving, and without any content that can be perceived. It follows that prior to diversity, without parts, there is only perceiving.

It's natural that the mind will want to explore where this wider viewing is coming from. If where we are looking from has an identifiable location, and if it had a starting moment, then viewing is not prior to the lens of time and space. Without the questions of where and when, the space-time lens can breakup. Let's leave the concept of space intact for now—it's fine if you detect or feel a sense of spacious-ness when you tune into your spiritual nature. Within the sense of spaciousness, timelessness, there is restfulness, stillness, ease, and peace. This is your spiritual nature, which is also called *non-duality*. Different spiritual traditions have their own words to point to non-duality. Whatever the term, you can know it by the fact that it won't readily have an opposite such as Absolute, God, stateless state, Self, pure awareness, emptiness, pure consciousness etc. Non-duality, a popular spiritual tradition in the west, derived from the Advaita schools in the east, asserts that your spiritual nature is non-dual and your true identity. You are the Source from which all else arises. That's true, and resonates internally as Truth, until it doesn't. Why? Because there really are no absolutes, just lenses of perception. The non-dual is also a lens of perception, albeit a critical one that marks awakening as a specific attainment along the path. We have an awakening experi-ence when we have a glimpse of non-duality. We know it because there is no personal in view; there is no "me" anywhere. What's important now is to let non-duality become familiar to you by hanging out there, so set aside time to tune into it, rest in it. According to the theory of non-duality, it is the final state, and resting attention in pure aware-ness is freedom. There is freedom, that's true, and yet there is more when one goes deeper than non-duality.

From both my personal and teaching experiences I've concluded that it's important to get very familiar with non-dual or pure awareness before going further so that our brains can adjust to perceiving and interpreting life in a new and different way. There are two things to do. We need to stabilize in our natural state, in pure, non-dual awareness, and learn how to detach from our other lenses of perception. Both steps are necessary.

Identification with the non-dual helps us to anchor in the natural state. Yes, we will have to discard the anchor further downstream, but for now it's both useful and necessary. If you don't first identify with the non-dual you will not be able to embody awakening because you will have skipped over a phase of integration whereby one settles into a normal usage of this important perspective. We need to embody and integrate awakenings in order to function in ordinary lives, to stay grounded, and to be practical.

Non-dual identification statements include "I am pure awareness," "I am pure consciousness," "I am the supreme consciousness," "I am That." Non-dual identification is not personal identification. But sometimes the personal masquerades as the non-dual. We can know this is happening when there is a personal agenda. Early indicators are that we feel puffed up or justified in our behavior.

PRACTICE: Statements of Identity that Are Not Personal

Relax your body and take some deep, slow breaths. Place one hand on your sternum and see if there is authenticity in this phrase as you say it aloud: "What I am is the Absolute, my true nature is pure, one and prior to all diversity." By comparison, as an experiment, let the personal I get off on the same idea. Engage the personal lens of perception and take your hand away from your breastbone. Let there be ownership over the following sentences: "I am the Absolute. I am the one, pure consciousness." Notice the difference? Feel the difference? Personal ownership feels different to non-dual identification. There is no personal I in the non-dual.

Now place one hand on your breastbone again and attune to your innermost nature. State this aloud and locate, in your chest area or in your heart, where it is true. "I am the Absolute, I am the one, pure consciousness."

PRACTICE: Identify with Non-Dual Awareness

Sense the personal "me" and detach by dropping deeper within. There isn't you and the non-dual because the concept of separation is not valid there. Identification with the non-dual feels like you are melting or merging into that from which you arose. The personal "me" disappears into the non-dual. You can sense your body and mind at a distance; don't be bothered with them now. Let yourself drop deeper into the spaciousness of the non-dual. Merge into it. Dissolve there. There is no "you" or "me," there is only spacious, non-dual, awareness.

Do you recognize that your experience of the world and your place in relation to it is an interpretation formulated by a lens of perception you are engaging? And do you see that your interpretation, your story about what is happening, is a subjective overlay superimposed on something that is perhaps much more straightforward? Do you know that how things are and how they appear to you could be two different things? Whatever your answers, inquire within to find out if you have implicit trust in personal stories, or can you be open to viewing the world and your own life differently? Can you be without stories? Can you be without your story? See if you can sense an internal shift, a letting go of familiar touchstones that are offered by the personal and impersonal lenses of perception.

Freedom comes when you live without reliance on any one lens of perception as a primary default way of perceiving. The paradigm that awaits you (or is already seen) requires you to recognize that lenses of perception are tools that your brain can pick up and set down as life demands. Your brain learns how to respond with an appropriate lens as it's needed in order to function effectively. You remain open and outside all story. There is expansiveness. You are looking from your true nature, the non-dual viewpoint. Internal dialogue that reinforces your separate position is not running. There is rest; mind is not labeling nor judging. It is quiet. There is peace and restfulness. Thoughts don't influence your behavior because their story content either doesn't attract your attention or is not compelling enough to enlist your support. You are capable of awakening other capacities within you.

Our path to freedom is without solid foundation until we have a working knowledge of when and how to pick up and set down the two primary lenses of perception (personal and impersonal). Spiritual maturation necessitates having the ability to be able to shift from one lens to another, as required by daily life. If we believe that one lens offers a more accurate viewpoint of the world, we will have a biased attachment that must be dropped. Our goal is objectivity and equanimity between these two perspectives.

It takes some effort to detach from the personal and impersonal lenses, especially as they have been the primary ways we viewed and interpreted the world until our spiritual path to awakening began. I'm asking you to change your relationship with what has brought you this far for something you can only discern in your body and vaguely sense in your brain. You have to trust your own inner knowing now. The next chapter asks questions that can help you track if you are still on this journey on a level that is deeper than your intellect.

I am aware that I'm using the story making mechanism (words, labels, etc.) to indicate that which is prior to story. Prior to story does not suffer from the absence of story; there is no sense of something missing. That would be another story. By its very nature, in the absence of all, it is fulfilled and complete with no option of an opposite state. Do you recognize that prior to all opposites is somehow intimately known to you? That's your spiritual nature.

CHAPTER 12

A Tale of Two Practices

A spiritual rebel has a binary spiritual practice: abidance and investigation. Abidance in one's spiritual nature means having an ongoing conscious awareness of your spiritual nature and investigation is the art of tidying up a messy, conditioned mind. This book helps you find your balanced blend of the two activities that best supports your spiritual evolution. The goal is to have an organic flow between both so that you can simultaneously be aware of your divinity and your humanity.

You can't abide in your spiritual nature if you don't know how to get there. Find out what helps you to be aware of your inner spiritual nature. There are many valuable traditional methods one can use to quiet the mind and body: to withdraw attention from personal "me" thoughts to impersonal observation, and deeper still, into your true nature. Once you place your attention on your spiritual nature, abidance begins. Abidance ends as soon as your attention is fully back in the world again. How to get your attention to your spiritual nature is trial and error for each of us. As you do the practices in this book, take note of what techniques are effective for you. You'll need to gather some tools to resource your own spiritual toolkit that can help you orient your attention to your spiritual nature quickly and efficiently. Routing your attention to your spiritual nature feels directional. For most, the direction is downward into the body, hence the phrase "dropping in." For others, taking the steps to shift lenses of perception from personal to impersonal to deeper than both lenses feels like where you are looking from is receding to the back of your head, and further still into a space behind your head. The phrases "pulling back" or "withdrawing your attention to where it came from" are tools in this case. For you, can you best access your spiritual nature by dropping in or by pulling back? Test out both and find out which is more effective for you.

Investigation is the art of figuring out why you can't sustain ongoing awareness of your spiritual nature. What is it that distracts you, engages you in personal drama? There is no value-derived hierarchy between abiding and investigation; don't create one. Welcome both as you would complementary tools like a knife and a fork. Be honest with yourself so that you are adept at recognizing which approach serves you better as your primary focus at any one time. Be comfortable with both. Be willing to interchange according to the demands of your unique spiritual path.

In my work as a spiritual teacher I have met quite a few people who have been meditating for over thirty years, yet they cannot attain ongoing, abiding inner peace in daily life because they haven't yet begun to investigate the subtle thoughts, beliefs, and values that influence and lock-in their lens of personal perception. Add in the belief that meditation is a more advanced spiritual practice than dismantling thinking processes and one is stuck like glue to a personal viewpoint that has potency for personal aggrandizement and spiritual ego.

Spiritual aspirants who dismiss the workings of the mind and choose not to investigate can, to some degree, awaken to the truth of their inner spiritual nature. They attain only a shallow and conceptual awareness. Their awakening experience was a glimpse of their inner nature, which can show up playing in present time from memory, and there is no authentic abidance. This is what I call a "neck-up awakening." Avoidance of getting down and dirty in the dissolution of personal beliefs and judgments because it is thought to be unnecessary is another idea that protects the self-perpetuating, subjective perspective. Those who have a neck-up awakening have limited understanding, lack wisdom and depth, and are unable to live their awakening. Embodiment is not achieved because the body and mind continue to hold experiences and desires. There is an absence of transparency. They cannot walk their talk. Invariably, there is unaddressed and most likely unrecognized fear underpinning this resistance to fully awakening.

Investigation is not therapy, though it can highlight a need for deep healing. At times it's possible that therapeutic approaches are required. Investigation is a form of psychological work, and it is necessary— not because something is wrong with us, but because something is right with us. Investigation is about challenging our beliefs and values. It's about being aware of our conscious and unconscious mind games and breaking their potency. I have also met many who have had a long term, sincere commitment to healing themselves and, because of the deep therapeutic work they have experienced, have access to advanced depths and insights into their spiritual nature. This is because when one is skilled at watching the subtleties of the mind, one develops an ability to recognize what would otherwise be unconscious or subconscious thoughts. There is no defense mechanism, personal agenda, nor justification because the personal lens is not personally owned.

When we are no longer willing to entertain personal drama, an inner depth is more accessible to us. This is an example of a mature approach to investigation. Our spiritual nature opens to us when we choose to withdraw allegiance from our minds. Abide and investigate.

CHAPTER 13

Out of Mind into Knowingness

Do you remember, as a child, having wisdom that you didn't or perhaps couldn't articulate? Did you at times have clarity around shortcomings of your parents, guardians, and teachers? Could you see simple and effective solutions that were not obvious to adults? All children incarnate with a wide lens of perception. Before the subjective filters overshadow and eclipse the light within, there is access to knowing, innocence, innate trust, and joy. Rekindle your access to that knowing with you. Tapping into innate knowingness is a tool that drops you right into your spiritual nature. Once there, rest and abide.

If you track the route into your own innate knowingness and you then feel an emotional response arising, let your emotions pass through you. How? Keep breathing and acknowledge your feelings. Don't suppress or deny, go towards an expansive feeling of openness within you. Touch into your inner knowing that was there prior to any experiences, prior to emotions in your memory.

Innate knowing doesn't know anything; it's not a store of knowledge. You could say it is knowledge itself. In resting your attention there, a calm confidence arises. Doubt, uncertainty, and grasping ceases. When life doesn't demand participation, it is still and silent. Rest your attention there. It's not a distracting, thought-filled space. There are no emotions at play. It's clear, simple, restful, and natural. Again, inner knowing doesn't necessarily know anything, and some find access to it by letting go of the need to know. When the mind is relaxed with "I don't know," the state of inner knowing can show up. Wisdom can then present, unbidden.

The state of innate, inner knowing is the same as the state of being. To rest in your own being, to simply be, are pointers to the same state. People tend to resonate with one word over the other. For me, the term "knowing" works better than "being" because I used to associate being as the opposite of doing. The association brought me back into the dual lens of either this or that. As soon as I would hear "just be" in a guided meditation, for example, my mind would say, *Ok, don't do anything*, which of course was my thinking mind going into story, making connections and trying to get it right. Being, or "simply be" as a directive didn't work for me. I choose knowing over being, though it may be that the word being is a better fit for you.

Practice withdrawing attention from thoughts and abide; hang out in knowingness. If one minute is the longest you can rest in knowingness, you are doing well. As your brain becomes familiar with the reorientation of your attention, you will learn how to speak and act from there. First the state of abidance must become familiar to your biology. You have to get used to inner peace. Difficulties can begin as soon as your thoughts and beliefs are given attention—that's what stops your peace. Watch for the emergence of the personal story mechanism and recognize its purpose without believing it to be the truth. Take it as your cue to turn down the volume of thoughts and turn your attention back to knowingness.

What if you can't abide there? Does your attention pop onto your thoughts after a couple seconds? If so, first train your brain to operate differently with short practices of abiding every day. Second, know that filters of perception were hard earned through the experiences that caused us to feel and believe we were unsafe, rejected, invisible, a target for abuse, or a victim of neglect. Whatever difficult experiences you have had, you are asked to choose freedom itself, not freedom from your experiences. However, by integrating and allowing your life to be included and held within your wider lens of perception, freedom itself is yours. Freedom has no hiding places. What is asking for investigation, understanding, and healing will vie for your attention. If you can't learn to abide with practice, then investigation is required. Investigation cannot be avoided if you are to live in radical freedom where your thoughts and actions are the uninterrupted impetus of your inner, spiritual, nature.

Revisiting the state of innate knowing is a route to abidance. Every spiritual path suggests methodologies that should be earnestly tried out so that you can gather your own tools that lead you to your spiritual nature, to pure consciousness. If you remember the state of knowingness from your childhood, you will know that life dragged you out of it, and spirituality now brings you back in touch with it. If abidance alone were all that was needed, then there would be nothing else to do now. You would look from and live from your spiritual nature. But life gives us mental habits, and we are not educated on how to use our minds well. It's never too late to learn how to use our minds well. Let our primary options be to either use a tool to abide in consciousness, or to investigate what compels our attention towards an obsolete and perhaps sufferable viewpoint.

PRACTICE: Through Knowingness to Abidance

Be still in your body by breathing slowly and relaxing your shoulders, belly, and legs. Tune into the sense of knowing that you had as a child. It is the sense of knowing that is present without any story of what you know. It is knowing itself. Once you can taste the destination, relax your body, settle in. Just one step deeper than knowingness, however *deeper than knowing* shows up for you, melt into it. Disappear.

CHAPTER 14

Integration

Innate knowingness is not a process of your brain. It is there prior to your brain's activity and your brain attunes to it as you become aware of it. Innate knowing is the glow of consciousness, your spiritual nature; it is one reality of spirituality.

PRACTICE: Consciousness with and without Awareness

Do you know you are conscious right now? Tune into the feeling, the sense that lets you know you are conscious. Now you are aware that you are conscious. Next, let consciousness be there without an awareness of it.

The starting point of creation is pure consciousness, and it becomes aware of itself in the very first movement. Self-awareness creates the potential for it to exist. Existence shows up as the ability to be, to know. Consciousness unfolds from one substance, remains as consciousness, showing up in the appearance of physical form.

Pure consciousness shows up as a brain with an ability to create thoughts, label, interpret, and manifest diversity. Your body (consciousness in form) houses your brain, and they work together to add credibility to your experience. Consciousness is everything, unfolding in progressively complex patterns which create what we see as opposites and diversity. Everything is consciousness; it's all one substance. Our lenses of perception create the diversity. Consciousness creates perceiving mechanisms (our brains) that allow it to experience itself in states of separation, yet it remains as pure consciousness. You need different lenses to live a human life. When we function as a balanced unit within our own body-mind structure, each lens has a part to play in enabling us to experience. Keep the wider view of consciousness as the backdrop to all that can show up whether your brain interprets what it perceives as real or imagined.

How you see the world is how your perception has created it. What you perceive is only a perception. When we share a perception, we say that thing is "true." However, consensus does not necessarily give a true or accurate representation of how things really are. Rather, it gives an experience which is derived from an interpretation. Your observations and interpretations create your experience. Whether you like what you experience or not is a preference, generated by your unique personal operating system. This is the production line of story making, generating a final product of a personal experience. The end of the line product (the me thought) will make you suffer if you attach to it or identify with it. Yet the end product is, always was, and always will be pure consciousness, playing as a separate being. If we believe our DMN, the "me" story makes us forget there is only pure consciousness at the core substance of everything. Recognize that perceptions generate new creations and different experiences from what is ultimately the same medium. By keeping the personal out of it, you can begin to perceive from a viewpoint that is further back on the production-line and prior to diversity.

Learning how to perceive from the wider viewpoint changes our experience of being human. Humanity is an expression of consciousness. Do not deny any experience. How experiences are registered is where the difference and potential for freedom lies, and is determined by the application (or not) of the personal perspective. Without the personal lens there is no "me and this," no "me and that" interpretation. It is in the absence of the believed thought of the personal me that our true nature shines.

Your personal belief system might advocate that you need to be in control and that nothing happens by itself. In fact, everything happens without you. That "you" is the obstacle that trades your innate divine wisdom for a personal story so that you can experience the drama of being with or without power, control, purpose, or meaning. Your true nature is not touched by any lens of perception. It is showing up as everything in every way it can.

PRACTICE: The Big How

1. Recognize each moment that your DMN is dominating your perception and experience of life.

2. Know that self-referencing is a personal creative process and, at best, a valid viewpoint for you only.

3. You have the ability to believe that your DMN perceptions are true and reality, or not.

4. Recognize that believing your DMN perceptions is self-hypnosis that ultimately creates suffering.

5. Let your human experiences have their place within a wider lens of perception.

6. Train your attention to abide in your spiritual nature, as pure consciousness, prior to subjective perceptions.

PRACTICE: Now What?

Abide as pure consciousness. Take the view from outside the personal story-making mechanisms. The character you play with their script and personality is seen without attachment. Your viewing point is not fixed to any lens of perception. Both the familiar (your comfort zone) and the unfamiliar are equal. You are not attached to any personal viewpoint.

A marker of integration is when everything and its opposite are both in view, while recognizing that only the personal can have a preference for one over the other. Personal preferences don't create contradiction. They are noticed and welcomed. Your personality can have a preference, but it will not be strong enough to exclude its opposite. We are dialing down the DMN, reducing the volume and not switching it off. The ability to perceive dualistically, to complete tasks and to enjoy stability in your life, are all set against the backdrop of pure consciousness. There is nothing wrong with any of it; we are finding freedom by rearranging all parts of us within a much broader landscape. From an integrated state you pick up the DMN as it is required, and you set it down afterward. Remain with some attention abiding as pure consciousness throughout.

CHAPTER 15

Consciousness

Science and spirituality differ in their opinions of consciousness. From a scientific perspective, the world is made of matter, and consciousness is a byproduct of matter. Spirituality holds the view that consciousness is prior to matter, that the world is consciousness *in matter*. From a spiritual perspective, everything is consciousness showing up in physical and ethereal forms. The traditional scientific view places validity on what can be measured or observed empirically. This approach naturally applies restrictions, limiting its arena to what can be explored only from the subject-object lens of perception. Spirituality, in contrast, asserts that there is a spiritual dimension to human beings and the universe. It has been my experience, without exception, that when someone who supports a mainstream scientific view has a spiritual experience of their own, they abandon their scientific beliefs and are drawn to finding out more about their spiritual, metaphysical nature. I've never known the opposite to happen. I've never seen anyone go back and discredit their spiritual awareness for a wholly materialist, scientific viewpoint.

My spiritual journey has shown me limitations in the non-dual teachings which advocate that there is nothing deeper than non-dual awareness, pure consciousness, the Absolute. I have found that this is not true. However, one can't dive deeper than the ancient non-dual teachings without having an everyday familiarity with non-dual awareness. Use the practices throughout this book to help you attune to and to abide in your natural state, resting as the pure, always singular Self.

Definition of Consciousness

Consciousness is the self-contained, self perpetuating capacity to manifest and experience itself as real or imagined. Consciousness is not created in your brain; your brain tunes in to it. Consciousness doesn't switch on and off; your brain tunes in and out of it. Your neural pathways determine your experience and awareness of consciousness. Even when you die, it remains.

Perhaps most of the time, your attention can be absorbed in the overlay of stories, offering stimulating diversity and distracting drama. When your brain is not aware of consciousness, nor abiding in consciousness, you are under the hypnotic spell of your personal thoughts. This happens a lot! While attention is caught up in stories, beliefs, and emotions, consciousness remains unchanged. Consciousness doesn't know that you are lost in your story because it doesn't do stories at all. Stories and judgments are created in our heads. From its point of view there is only itself. It doesn't do separation or diversity. It is the subject, and all is the subject because there is only itself, the subject. It doesn't need the physical body or anything for it to be what it is.

For as long as we continue to believe our thoughts, it will remain impossible to see and recognize that consciousness is the substratum of everything. When we believe our thoughts, there is separation and diversity. Literally, your experience depends on where you are looking from. If you are looking from your brain, there's one of two views. Either there is a personal story interpreting, or there is a wider relaxed observation filtering every moment. Does consciousness perceive something? It isn't *that* active. For now, it's wise to recognize that consciousness is; it doesn't do. It is more about *being* than *doing*.

In earlier chapters we have used the term "spiritual nature." For now, we can equate your spiritual nature with consciousness because, so far, it's the deepest spiritual point we have explored. Later we go deeper than consciousness, leaving the theory of non-duality behind. That next step will be an intellectual exercise unless you are first familiar and solid in your awareness of consciousness. Why? Because your brain must be retrained so that your lenses of perception are rendered to their original, optimal functions. You will need to practice picking up and setting down a lens of perception, as required by life's circumstances. Make a conscious effort to retrain your brain to work efficiently and properly. The goal is to no longer be invested in, attached to, or readily believing your mind. Like any other physical organ your brain will create new muscle memory and automatically function in the new pattern in time.

At first it is mentally cumbersome to shift from one lens of perception to another, to remember to see the wider view, observe your thoughts, drop the personal agenda, and rest within. It sounds like a whole lot to do. It's worth it. After a while old habits no longer compel or influence your behavior.

Day-by-day, try to become more aware of where you are looking from. Learn to identify where you are looking from, that is, when are you engaging your DMN, when you are hanging out and living from the impersonal viewpoint? Fearless freedom, our ultimate goal, is when you are viewing from somewhere that is deeper than both. How is your TON? Can you perform tasks independent of any personal thoughts? By retraining your brain, your DMN doesn't need to switch off; it's enough if the volume reduces and you retain an objective awareness about when and how it becomes active. The abidance component of a spiritual rebel's binary practice is easier than investigation. Read on; there is help available.

CHAPTER 16

Get out of Your Own Way

Fred first came to me having had a new spiritual experience. He wanted to understand what caused his experience, and whether it should be ignored or used in some way to enhance his spiritual awareness. Fred was committed to a daily practice of watching his thoughts without judgment for some years, and an intermittent meditator. He was a schoolteacher by profession.

One day at work, Fred was called into the principal's office, so he stilled his mind and dropped his attention within. He had wanted to calm his nervous system and set an intention to be present, disengaging in any mind chatter. He considered the idea that he should adopt a role that would project his professional persona but cast that aside, choosing empty, open availability instead. He was managing his state of mind when he felt something open within him. There was a shift from exploring a state of mind to an absorbing of his attention into pure consciousness. He was aware that he was looking from a place deeper than mind. No thoughts, only absolute calmness. The natural fluidity of life itself was making life happen. He felt disarmed walking to the office, but not unsafe. What followed was an open, productive, and professional meeting. It was a simple and easier process than any other meeting he had ever had. He told me that the content of the meeting was an organic exchange, rich and complete within the totality of the present moment.

Neither he nor I know how his boss experienced Fred that day. Whatever lenses of perception were influencing her experience met no resistance in Fred. When we come from pure consciousness our openness and honesty is steeped in humility. The environment we help create becomes non-threatening for others: no games, no projections, no judgments. Being available and fully present is primary, and, in the absence of any personal agenda, our exchanges with others are free to play out in honest openness. Fred had never before had an interaction like this with another person. He told me he realized that he never truly saw the woman who had been his boss for six years. He recognized that what he had formerly believed about her was not accurate at all. He realized that he didn't know anything about her because he had readily believed the fabrication his mind had created. Anxiety and projections had manifested a rich story about her that was very different to the reality of who she is. What happened for Fred prior to his meeting was that, instead of observing his thoughts as was his normal practice, his viewpoint separated from the filter lens that created his thoughts. He didn't just pull back from the story content of thoughts; he pulled back from the mechanism that created thoughts. His subjective filters of perception were not influencing his experience. He was in his natural state perceiving as pure consciousness. He told me that he was aware of the sense of perfection throughout the experience, perfection that was independent to how the meeting unfolded. Whatever the content of the meeting, he said, the perfection could not be affected.

By getting out of his own way and being fully present (not using personal filters or relying on a role), a fresh and authentic version of the world came into Fred's view. Was Fred now trying to grasp the experience in order to repeat it? His mind had made a memory of it and was setting up the experience as a phenomenal repeatable state. A subtle approach is needed. The lenses of perception in our minds are an overlay on pure consciousness. They are not a problem unless their filtering function is believed to help you discern what is the truth. The shift comes in the recognition that you are not tied to the viewpoint of your DMN. The willingness to spiritually grow must be greater than the motivation to protect and uphold the personal "me." Your trusted defense mechanism, your personal identity, is set aside. You are open and available; you are present.

Fred's opening of his perception continued to widen. As he worked to keep it open, his skills of observation deepened. He was looking forward to meeting friends and family to see if he would meet familiar people for the first time, in the perfect present.

PRACTICE: Get out of Your Own Way

Have love and compassion for your personal character. Be gentle with it. Don't kill it off. Instead lay it to rest. In doing so, you are shifting your viewpoint from the personal *all about me* perspective to a much more expansive viewpoint of your spiritual nature. Zoom out. Get distance and withdraw your attention from the self-generating network. Recognize the objectivity and clarity derived from viewing the mechanism that creates the personal "me" story. Now withdraw your attention. Pure consciousness has no story. It's a place to look from.

As long as you believe your personal character gives you essential currency, credibility, and identity, then you will unquestionably adopt its position. As you grow spiritually, greater value and meaning are derived from an internal sense of harmony and wellbeing. You come to recognize that the personal "I" can't deliver anything of true value. The only thing that needs to be changed now is your viewing point. The personal has to get out of the way of your spiritual nature. If the personal self negatively views itself with criticism, judgment, or self-doubt the personal paradigm is still at play. If you view the personal impersonally, there is no commentary. The personal lens of perception is seen for what it is: a useful tool for managing in the world. Cease judgments. Your personal sense of self isn't the issue; it's the habitual belief in it that requires changing. Now is not the time to invest in a new definition of yourself. External distractions like having an affair, buying luxury toys, or falling victim to a midlife crisis won't help. Investing in your definition of yourself in any of these ways is an immature, unhealthy option that will only postpone what is, in reality, a beautiful inner-growth spurt.

PART 4

THE INFLUENCE OF PAIN

CHAPTER 17

In Support of Investigation

When I was preparing the first draft of this book, my publisher asked me to make the material useful and relevant for people who might be new to the spiritual path. I asked them to describe my reader, and the profile they outlined didn't match that of my students. *I don't think they are my audience. I don't think I have anything useful to offer to this reader.* The publishers made suggestions on how to envisage my readership, and I again couldn't connect with their ideas. They asked me to remember what it was like for me when I was starting off my journey, but I can't remember what it felt like. It has been too long since I was seeking, and way too long since I first became interested in spirituality. I can't remember my experience of life before. Months went by, and I was unable to write a word. I perceived my ideal reader and the publisher's target audience as two very different sectors.

My husband is on his spiritual path too. As you might guess, living with me is not for the faint of heart. Early on in our relationship we were living between two continents, and our visits to each other were intense and wonderful. One time he arrived in Ireland, very enthusiastic about his proximity to a teacher (me, his girlfriend), and he said, "For these 2 weeks, whatever you can see in me that needs some work please point it out to me." That didn't work, not even a little bit. I learned that though we are willing, it's often not enough. There is a timing issue that we must honor. We can only unravel an old habit or uncover a blind spot when they are ready to be seen. Issues have to run their course.

During my unable to write phase of this book, my husband was going through a difficult time on his own journey. I know now that when he is caught in a story, it's best that I don't tell him what I see. I steer clear of him, and I let him figure things out on his own unless he asks for my intervention on something he has specifically identified as an issue for him. Still, I could see what he was going through from the tightness in his face from deep emotional pain. Then I put the pieces together. I was living with the publisher's readership! I decided to write down what I thought would be helpful for my husband to know. I created the middle section of this book, in the name of investigation, and I showed it to him for spelling and grammatical review. "Great material," he said. "This is so useful for what's going on with me right now." He was now finding distance from his own pain. It could have been read as intellectual material, but something in him was ready to let go and to move beyond his pain. Without him knowing it, he was ready for resolution and healing. I found my ideal reader, at least of the middle part of the book! Thank you for your journey, dear Derek.

Whether the following chapters resonate as your story or not, let them move and stir up what they will within you. The process of healing ourselves remains open throughout our lives. Each time I move to live in a new country or teach in an unfamiliar culture, I get to see a whole new set of conditioned ideas and assumptions that I never knew were in me. I enjoy the challenge, the confusion, and the feeling of misalignment as they present. Discovering new blind spots stirs an enthusiasm for my own growth and evolution as a human being. When a big change comes in my life, such as a death, shift in a primary relationship (having children would be included if I were a parent), someone moving in or moving out of my home, serious health issues, changing jobs, or moving, it can bring up new challenges. Spiritual progress doesn't automatically take care of our human development. Changes in my personal life bring the opportunity for investigation, for paying attention to my emotional wellbeing, for psychological inquiry. My journey has taught me to celebrate psychological change: my own growth process.

CHAPTER 18

Emotional Intelligence

Do you give too much power to your emotions? Do you make decisions based on emotions? Do your emotions stop you from being assertive and performing well? Do you get anxious or tongue tied? Cultivate an awareness of the role of emotions in your daily life.

Awareness of how you experience and use emotions is essential to your spiritual growth. In this chapter we will explore the practice of recognizing your thoughts and your emotions as separate functions in order to better manage both. Doing so is the key to increasing your emotional intelligence.

In earlier chapters we looked at how thoughts about "me," coupled with an emotion, create and reinforce the self-referencing DMN. When you have habitual thoughts, know that it is indicative of repeatedly using the same neural pathways. When your mind is caught up in repeating thoughts, you are not observing what is creating rumination, and you are not conscious of your spiritual nature. You are identifying with a lens of perception and engaging in whatever content matter it is producing. You are playing small, imagining you are your body and your thoughts. You are not present. Furthermore, if you have an emotion entangled with a thought, you reinforce the neural circuitry that gives rise to that thought.

Neuroscientists frequently use the term "hardwiring" to describe the neural circuitry associated with habitual thinking patterns. I have found that the use of the term "hardwiring" is inaccurate; there is nothing *hard* about the brain. Our brains are dynamic organs of soft tissue that can, with direction, repair themselves from many diseases (and thinking patterns) that formerly were thought irreversible. Nothing is physically fixed or hardwired in your brain.

Repeating a thought reinforces the habit of thinking that thought, and a repeated thought becomes a belief. Your DMN is without a capacity to discern the truth content of thoughts. It readily makes associations and assumptions, and it reinforces beliefs. Whatever your DMN tells you about you and your experiences is taken literally, and these thoughts are also automatically believed to be true. When we support a personal thought with an emotion, we add a value to the content of the thought. Now we have something to invest in: a belief. Beliefs connected to our value system support our personal identity and can be difficult to see through.

PRACTICE: Criticism and Emotions

Think of a negative characteristic about your personal character. Now hold this critical point in your mind. Did an emotion arise, unbidden, to couple with the negative thought? If an emotion readily showed up when you focused on a negative aspect of your personality, it tells us that your brain's self-referencing network is using your emotions to corroborate a story about you. Neural wiring that readily joins emotions with opinions results from a bad habit that most of us learn in childhood. We use this technique when training dogs. When a dog obeys a command, we create an association in them between their behavior and an emotion by giving them a tasty reward. We are conditioning habitual behavior by linking it to a positive feeling. The same has happened to us. Take a few deep breaths with the intention of releasing any emotions arising. Keep breathing until there is calmness in your body again and all emotion has dissipated.

Now bring the negative attribute about you to mind again, and do not offer attention to your emotions. Let the negative aspect be seen, to be recognized as the piece of data that it is. If you didn't have an emotional response, if you naturally held an objective non-critical viewpoint while identifying a negative, then well done!

PRACTICE: Nonemotional Data

Now bring to mind someone you don't like. Name the characteristics that you dislike. Let your opinion be objective data. Keep your thoughts and your emotions apart. Don't engage an emotion. Exercises like these help cultivate emotional intelligence.

If you experienced an emotion with the negative thought, we can know that the thought is believed to be true, and that you used your DMN for the exercise. In so doing, a memory bank of previously generated emotions supplied credibility and self-referencing potency. Your emotions when used by the DMN are an innately trusted historical catalogue that helps consolidate a habitual, familiar idea of you. That's how the DMN builds an identity of you. Except it's not you. You only need a sense of the personal mainly to be able to communicate, to engage boundaries for healthy functioning, and to manage and enjoy your body. The problems come when we take the DMN's idea of you to be who you really are. The persona as presented by your DMN is not *you*. Your brain cannot create your identity. If you didn't use your DMN for either exercise, you would have been in benign observation mode, objectively naming an aspect of your personality that needs refinement. The exercises would not be personal.

Practice shifting your perspective so that both yours and others' negatives are named without emotion, judgment, nor criticism. Thus, you will remove some reinforcements of emotion that support your DMN. When there is a negative thought without an emotion, you are poised to examine if it's true or not. You will develop tolerance, objectivity, and acceptance without judgment or criticism. If there is no emotion and you are not denying or suppressing emotions, you are having an impersonal thought and not using your DMN. You have now proven that you can engage your brain in a new way and establish new neural pathways. It's a healthier use of your mind to see your positive and negative attributes without emotion.

My spiritual path has shown me that there is freedom when self-referencing ceases. I also know from personal experience that the most potently addictive thoughts can cease permanently. Some thoughts or patterns of thinking return post-awakening. The primary differences are that they are no longer automatically connected to emotion and are not readily believed.

Thoughts without emotion have no potency; they can't hold your attention for more than a fleeting moment. If a post-awakening stream of thoughts were compared to a radio show, it would be comparable to an innocuous conversation at an almost inaudible volume. If I were to fully invest my attention in the external world again, if I were to believe that worldly things would bring a quality of lasting happiness greater than what I experience within, it's very likely that my DMN would reconstruct itself in order to support these thoughts. The brain is a healthy organ constantly regenerating neural pathways. The spiritual path is an ongoing journey.

CHAPTER 19

Cultivating Emotional Intelligence

This chapter is about changing your relationship with your emotional capacity. The goal is to manage your emotions so that they no longer have the power to consume your attention at the cost of abiding in your true spiritual nature.

Emotions are natural to our human condition; they arise, seek expression, and are released. With emotional intelligence, emotions move through our body system quickly, leaving no residue behind. Your spiritual path helps you to create enough bandwidth of attention to maintain a conscious awareness of the zone that is deeper than all stories, while fully feeling an emotion as it finds expression. Your spiritual nature doesn't deny emotion. Learning how to feel and express emotions and not get lost in them brings freedom. Then, emotions are not co-opted or used by the DMN to forward a personal agenda. There is no indulgence in emotion.

If your emotional capacity is easily activated there are three areas to explore so that we can cultivate emotional intelligence. This is not an exhaustive list, but it's a good place to begin. The three areas are: learned habits from childhood, emotions from memory and values with emotion.

Childhood

In your childhood, did you use your emotional states as your safe and familiar refuge? Did you use your emotions to get attention? Did they help you to be seen and heard? Did you manipulate with your emotions? If you can answer positively to any of these questions, then as an adult your emotions will most likely hold a disproportionate value. If this is so, you will give them too much significance, and how you feel will command excessive attention. As a result, your emotions will disproportionately influence your decision making by obscuring your interpretation of actions and interactions. Emotions are expressions. They are not to be used as tools to satisfy desires. Doing so reinforces identification with the self-referencing network. What I encourage is that you surrender your childhood place of safety, that you allow maturation in your use of emotions, and that you welcome a change in your emotional experience. No one can make you feel emotions. No one can make you feel shame, guilt, or anger. Emotions are created by you and are within your control. With the proportionate use of emotions, your perception of circumstances will be more honest and objective.

Practice communicating without emotions. Your awareness will notice emotions beginning to bubble as they vie for your attention. Resistance will arise. Continue with the practice in spite of your doubts and reluctance. Remember to breathe. Emotions dissipate with deep breathing. Emotion is released on the out-breath, while shifting attention to your breath reduces indulgence in emotions.

PRACTICE: Communicate in Calmness

Work towards developing the skill to communicate without internal emotional interference. Anchor your communication in a calm, centered, objective presence. Communicating in this manner is not complicated; it's natural. You are present, your attention is available to respond to what is happening. Love is present within you. If you are not aware of the presence of love within you then old thinking habits and beliefs are obscuring your access to it. Love is integral to the natural state. In the absence of distraction from the mind, there is love. From your calm and balanced center, should other emotions arise they are a natural response that is proportionate to what is happening in that moment. Don't draw from old patterns of behavior or learned responses. Because you are present you are attentive and really listening.

Emotions and Memory

If you already know how you will feel in a given scenario, you are living in emotional memory. You are drawing from an old template, from a past experience, and the simple act of being present is no longer available to you. There is neither growth nor joy when every situation is another version of a rerun. There is nothing dull or boring about being present. Every moment is fresh and rich with new experience when you are not filtering your interpretation of what is happening with historical emotional content. Retrain your thought patterns and your brain will adjust its circuitry. Cultivating new patterns is essential for a smooth sustained awakening to your divine spiritual nature.

PRACTICE: Be Present

Mindfully respond to every present moment situation without self-referencing from memory or adding emotional embellishments.

Emotions and Values

Thoughts with a moral content stir the greatest emotional reaction. Is your value system linked to your emotions? It is difficult for most to speak about politics, violence, or the environment without stimulating emotions. Notice how you readily couple an emotion with your viewpoint when you think of something being right or wrong. Having the ability to separate data from your feelings and decision making from your emotions when engaging with moral, social, political, and familial issues is emotional intelligence in action. Because emotions are learned, you can relearn how to better use them. By removing the emotional charges attached to your beliefs and values, you will gain tolerance, understanding, and acceptance. Your passion will survive. With emotional maturity you can be loyal to what you uphold without emotional sabotage. Without distortion from your emotions, you will have the capacity to be present and fully hear your most opposing point of view. Decouple your emotions from your position of right and wrong. Wisdom comes when we can calmly walk a mile in the shoes of another, even when we don't hold the same values.

When emotions are not poised to react, you are more aware of your internal emotional experience. Emotions are not denied; they are observed and released.

PRACTICE: Identify your Emotional Triggers

Take note of who or what situations trigger emotional reactions. Notice what media images stimulate an emotional response. As you recognize emotional triggers around you, take a breath and let your exhale be longer than your inhale. Repeat this breathing pattern four or five times. This is one way you can manage your emotions and calm them down as you return your body to a less emotional state. Know that your awareness is developing, and celebrate that you are no longer being played by your emotions. If you do this your autonomy will increase. Your wisdom will increase. Attention that would otherwise be used up with the experience of emotion will be made available to what is happening in this present moment. Such is the natural order of healthy thinking coupled with emotional intelligence.

If you have been alive long enough to know that it's pointless to try to gain control of people and most circumstances around you, draw comfort from the wisdom of knowing what you cannot change. What is within your control is the way you interpret and respond to life's circumstances in any given moment. If you increase your awareness of your emotional experience, you will find that you will respond to what presents in an open manner instead of reacting and reinforcing your DMN. Put your attention on what you can change. Stop responding from an emotional, personalized interpretation. Instead exercise an objective interpretation of your actions and interactions and be available and open to respond in the moment.

When you cultivate skills that manage your emotions there is attentive space for love to arise.

CHAPTER 20

Overwhelm

Overwhelm is emotional distress. In the state of overwhelm we are under pressure because what is expected of us is greater than our resources. It makes us inefficient and ineffective. It is not a desired state that helps us to work better; it's a learned response. Overwhelm happens when emotions crank up to the point where we feel distressed. Overwhelm is when our bodies are pulled into our personal, emotional story of that moment. At this point we have lost objectivity and the view is personal, supported by a physiological chemical charge that goes with emotional distress. Like all emotions, overwhelm is a learned response.

If you experience overwhelm, know that it is taxing on both your body and your mind, leaving insufficient energy and focus for you to perform well. You feel alone; it's hard to place your attention on one thing. Your physical movements are hurried and erratic. You need your resources to function optimally. If overwhelm is not managed, it can spiral into a cycle of stress and distress and becomes a habitual way of being. It can grow stronger, further disempowering you from what you want to do. When you are in emotional distress (overwhelm), you are lost in your experience. Heightened emotions do not help us to become more efficient. They help the DMN reinforce personal identification using stress-producing chemicals to support beliefs around a personally viewed situation.

In order to break the habit of feeling overwhelmed we must look at beliefs. *Beliefs* are ideas you have taken as facts; they are imprisoning you with limiting attitudes, rules, and behaviors. For example, do you believe that you should be able to do everything, that you should be able to meet everyone's expectations? It's time to stop dragging your past into the present. Stop hauling your beliefs with you. Whether beliefs are genetic, adopted in childhood, or learned from life's experiences, someone somewhere believes the opposite of what you hold to be true. Beliefs are not right or wrong when it comes to spirituality. Our task is to free ourselves from their grip by identifying them and understanding how they bind our thinking processes. Habits are based on conscious and unconscious beliefs. Breaking the habit of feeling overwhelmed is a multilayered process.

PRACTICE: Stress, Distress, and Overwhelm

Identify your beliefs around your own personal efficacy. What do you honestly believe is your contribution and its value? Make a list. Bring your belief system to your awareness in written form. It will help to expose the roots of old habits that hide out in your subconscious. Your habits are based on your beliefs. Aim for honest self-exposure. Your written beliefs might include statements such as: *When I'm very busy I feel important and useful, I like having lots of things to do, I feel stress because I believe I'm not doing enough, I love the buzz that comes with stress, I feel guilty if I don't give my maximum, I secretly think I am a superhero, nobody will help me, I'm not able to ask for help, I should be able to accomplish more on my own*, etc. Whether these examples are valid for you or not, use them to help you explore your personal beliefs around your value and contribution. Be honest with yourself; the beliefs that must be unearthed now could be ones you won't want to admit to.

Now look at your list. Do you see how your beliefs restrict you? Look at each belief individually and be with what it would feel like to be without that specific belief. Give your body and mind a few minutes to enter the space of being without each belief. This space is going to be your new normal. Spend some time getting used to it. Now make the decision to no longer support your list of beliefs. Is that too high a jump? No, it isn't; your intention is what will make this happen.

This practice helps create new neural pathways as you untangle your emotions from your sense of self by no longer judging your efficacy. In the absence of beliefs, your true nature is available. Take some time to rest in the inner calmness, which always lies beneath superimposed beliefs, habits, and behavior. Notice what emotion arises; don't change it, just notice. A sense of relief can come as you recognize the limitations you've unnecessarily placed on yourself. A sense of spaciousness may be experienced at this stage of the exercise. Don't grab any experience; stay open. Don't make this experience bad or good, right or wrong. Remain open and at ease.

Fearless freedom will not come from swapping out one set of beliefs for another. Fearless freedom is the original template, the core of your being that was never touched or tarnished by your hard earned beliefs, traumas, and stories. In spite of your life's experiences, it remains the same as always.

CHAPTER 21

Emotional Balance

Early on my spiritual path I came to the recognition that when my emotions were activated, I was caught up in the story of "me." When I would have an emotional reaction, I had no access to my spiritual nature or the impersonal objective viewpoint. Emotional reactivity was a full-on expression of the personal me. I needed to dial down my emotions. Not to suppress or deny them, but to bring them into balance. I knew I would reduce the number of triggers that activated my self-referencing habits if I was less reactive.

Some emotions are a natural response. With these I could remain present and aware. They added some color to my experience. Other times when the personal was activated I might react, be combative, or find myself swept away by my own emotional reaction. I needed to recognize the difference between emotional reactions and natural emotional responses.

I decided the best course of action was to stop all emotional reactions. And it worked! I began by repeating to myself, "Don't have an emotional reaction." I would say this sentence over and over throughout each day and after some weeks the wisdom of the sentence had an impact on my thought-to-emotion sequence. Repetition is an effective strategy. It is proactive brain conditioning. At first, I would notice emotions were activated. With noticing, I would drop the emotion, calm my body, and continue without the heightened response.

The statement "don't have an emotional reaction" is restrictive and negative for some, but it isn't for me. When I figure out what I need to do to support my growth, I feel empowered. I don't care what the tool is, I'm not bothered if it is punitive in another context. That doesn't distract me. I didn't feel restricted by "don't have an emotional reaction," I felt empowered by the change it could bring about in me. Everybody is different. If you had a negative response to "don't have an emotional reaction," then honor that. What tool can you use that holds your resolve to be present and aware instead of spiraling into emotional reactions? Find your phrase. Examples to consider are one word anchors such as "calmness," "balance," "objectivity," or, if you're feeling ambitious, you can try affirmative phrases that ignite identification with your spiritual nature, such as "I am pure consciousness," "I am divine," or "I am awareness," Whatever you choose, your phrase should not be negotiable. Remember that it's purpose is to reroute your attention to inner-equilibrium.

The moment you become aware that an emotional reaction has taken over or is about to pop up, use your word or phrase and withdraw. In practice this could mean pulling out of an argument regardless of whether you are on the winning or losing side. It might mean lowering the pitch or the volume (or both) of your voice while in mid-sentence because you just recognized that you lost it with your kids. Do you want to win a battle or to leave the war? Do you want to be right, or do you want to be happy? The second you recognize that you are caught in emotional drama, pull out of it. If you do this, you will recognize earlier each subsequent time when you are caught up in emotional drama.

After a few days of constantly repeating "don't have an emotional reaction," I began to notice a subtle flow of chemicals in my body that were setting up an emotional reaction. I had stopped reacting outwardly, but chemicals were still triggered. My thoughts were activating a neuroendocrine surge that is a prerequisite to experiencing emotion. I had to go deeper. I continued with "don't have an emotional reaction," using it as one would use a mantra. I repeated it when I was alone, every hour I remembered to do so. I gained new insight into the store of personal beliefs and ideas that gave rise to the reactions. Wanting to be right was at the top of my list. I listed and dissolved my attachment to these beliefs.

Within a month my awareness was acute to the point of arresting the emotional reaction by noticing an underpinning belief, which I would simply smile at it. *Almost caught me again*, I'd say. The production line was clear to me; personal "I" beliefs co-opted the body into producing chemicals which found expression in emotional reactions. If I kept attention away from "me" stories, none of this emotional turbulence would arise. Once I broke the chain reaction, I kept repeating the sentence "don't have an emotional reaction" off and on for about a year. This might seem excessive, but in its defense the practice brought much freedom. Without emotional reactions my awareness stayed with what was happening, identification with the personal "I" significantly reduced; there weren't long periods where I got lost in my story. Emotional reactions are an interference that block authentic emotional expressions. In hindsight I was weakening a fundamental neural circuit that supported my DMN.

If you live a full and busy life, you will need to add one other practice to maximize the freedom that comes from effective emotional management. You will need to pay attention to how much of each day is reactive versus proactive. Personal technology is training our brains to be reactive. Do you, for example, begin your day by seeing what's in your email inbox or on social media, and do you instantly engage by reacting to what appears on your device? If so, you are training your brain to be reactive. Emotional reactivity is then a symptom of a deeper unhealthy patterning. You cannot intercept emotional reactions if you are conditioning your brain to be primarily reactive on a daily basis.

Habitually wiring yourself daily for reactivity keeps your attention turned outward. An outward focus will lead you to increasingly seek stimulation from the external world, in which case your brain will not remember the ease and rest of inner peace. The inner world will be less familiar, and it will seem at least boring when you are unconsciously watching out for an external stimulus. Making sure that you can rest in a state that is relaxed and still, without distractions, is important.

PRACTICE: Nonreactive Time

Set aside time every day where you do not engage with personal technology. For your health and your spiritual evolution, the best time to do this is first thing in the morning, from the moment you awaken. Let two hours of living happen before you turn on your phone or computer. As you adjust to natural calmness include more nonreactive spaces in every day. Become familiar and feel comfortable without external stimuli.

If you don't take this step and you check a personal device numerous times a day, you will lose the skill to be at rest within. Resting your attention within is essential for awakening to truth. There is no freedom to be had when your mind is searching for distractions to avoid what lies within. Break this habit; it's worth it! There is nothing in the external world that can bring you true and lasting freedom.

PART 5

BREAKING FREE FROM LIMITATIONS

CHAPTER 22

Moving Beyond Trauma

In this chapter, you are invited to check-in with yourself and enquire if there is unresolved trauma in your life story. It's time to find out if your mind or your body is retaining impact from trauma that you have experienced. However, please note that identifying and acknowledging this impact might be as far as we can go in this book because healing trauma is a specialized field.

Trauma is a legitimate response to many life events. One can have trauma from falling off a bicycle in addition to the more obvious causes of abuse and neglect. Traumatic experiences affect our bodies as well as our minds. When there is trauma, the sympathetic nervous system is co-opted. The phrase "fight or flight" is in common usage. Yet we rarely hear about "rest and digest," the phrase that describes the normal and calm body-mind state. Rather than the more passive rest and digest mode that is a function of the parasympathetic nervous system, the sympathetic nervous system is on standby, in case we need to fight or flee. The sympathetic and parasympathetic nervous systems are part of the autonomic nervous system which controls bodily functions that are not consciously directed (e.g. breathing, digestion etc.). Past experiences (particularly ones that were often repeated) may have determined that the fight or flight response is more appropriate than a rest and digest option. Even if your mind knows you are now safe, your body can support another story from memory.

If there is trauma in your body, it will have to be acknowledged and softened before fearless freedom can be the new normal way of being. When the nervous system is free from the impact of trauma, it can rest in the natural state as the mind attunes to pure consciousness.

Our goal is to return your body to its original blueprint, its natural state. What would the natural state, the blueprint of your body be like? Do you have healing and releasing work to do to bring your body there?

If you are unsure whether your body is holding trauma, the content of your self-talk is another indicator of unresolved trauma. In an attempt to remain safe, the rhetoric of the DMN becomes the voice of a mind-created enemy. Thoughts like *I knew I'd be no good at that, I'm worthless, nobody is interested in me, nobody gets me, I'm a bad person, I'd rather not be alive* are examples of trauma held in the body that shows up as narrative running in the DMN.

It is true that you can overcome every experience you have had, no matter how traumatic. Nothing can stop freedom from breaking through once your determination and commitment is in place. Managing the mind and ignoring the role of the body when it is holding memories of personal, painful stories will enable a neck-up or shallow awakening. Such spiritual realizations will be intellectual and inauthentic and will prove unsustainable over time. It's not possible to have an embodied awakening in a traumatized body. The good news is that you can heal your past traumas.

PRACTICE: Rest and Digest

Activate the rest and digest state by relaxing your body. Let your out-breaths be longer than your in-breaths. Drop your interest in mind chatter. Pay attention to your body and begin to notice when there is tension. Don't buy into the physical reaction of tension, flight or fight. Watch it instead. Let it be there. Acceptance can help the process of dissolving tension. Next slow down your breathing so that the rise and fall of your chest are slower. Use your breath to relax your body. Switch your attention to rest and digest. In telling your body to rest and digest, you are giving it a new response. You are retraining, aligning it with the present moment instead of supporting memory. Bring your awareness into the state where you are resting and digesting. In this way you can use your mind to help activate the parasympathetic system.

CHAPTER 23

Inside Out

Have you spent your life trying to be what other people told you to be? Have you followed an external model of how to be? Have you made choices because others expected or coerced you to take a specific path? The susceptibility to be externally controlled is a symptom of low self-worth. If you have received lots of direction from external sources on how to live you will not have a familiarity with getting direction from within.

Fearless freedom requires our minds, our bodies, and our hearts to be in alignment with our spiritual nature. Alignment means no inner conflict and that our humanity supports and serves our divine nature in full transparency and integrity. Direction comes from within. You can discern and recognize an inner impetus as the flow of life itself, the natural order of the universe. If you are wired to take your lead from external sources, you are inside out. When inner direction comes you will buckle; there will be conflict.

If your monitor for success is grounded in acceptance from others you can feel self-doubt or paralysis when faced with decisions, because you have not activated your own inner compass. There will be fear, and you will want to run your choices by those to whom you have given authority. Your reference points must come from inside you. You will make plenty of mistakes until you cultivate the wisdom to listen clearly and honor your own inner direction. Even then you'll continue to make mistakes, albeit with less frequency, and you will learn from the experiences they offer. The fear and judgment that goes with making mistakes disappears with the personal "I." Mistakes are viewed positively by your inner nature offering a new experience for growth and attaining wisdom. Speaking to others about what you are doing will give you a second opinion. You can assess the usefulness of their opinions. Whether they approve or not is no longer of interest to you.

PRACTICE: Self-Autonomy

Start making decisions on your own and be curious as to what the outcome might be. An attitude of curiosity is key to this exercise. By taking this approach you will develop new skills that will increase your self-worth, confidence, and autonomy. It's not about getting it right. It is about deciding without self-referencing and following it through with action. Self-autonomy is inner decision that leads to outer action. Learn to trust yourself and follow through on your own ideas and gut feelings. Embrace learning and growth and enjoy the expansion and confidence that comes with it.

CHAPTER 24

Self-Acceptance

You don't need other people to accept you—you only need to accept yourself. If you choose to take this necessary step and accept yourself, whether others reject or accept you will not have a high impact on you. It's something that happens on the periphery of your field of vision whereas before, when filtering through the DMN, we can feel rejection like a physical punch in the gut. You will interpret how others react towards you as a curious amusement because unconditional self-acceptance takes you out of the DMN's mind games. With authentic self-acceptance, how you relate to yourself, how you perceive yourself, and how you treat yourself grow rich with tenderness and love. Feeling less than when you compare yourself to others—imagining you are somehow not enough, that you are unworthy—arises from negative beliefs about yourself. Accept yourself exactly as you are right now. Let how and who you are be good enough for you. No one else's opinions need impact on your relationship with yourself. It is your DMN that advocates otherwise in an effort to create an identity for you. Be done with games of the mind, and rest in total unqualified self-acceptance.

When we believe we need acceptance from others, our self-perception is distorted. If we harbor the belief that there is an ongoing threat of rejection, the impact on us is that we believe we are inherently less than. We do not have to be a certain way for us to survive, to give and receive love. If we believe we are less than, we will be needy, always trying to fill the gaps within ourselves. If you have a habit of feeling needy or acting out from a needy place, you'll want to drop the habit. When we are needy, we can't cultivate self-authority and autonomy. Neediness stifles courage and promotes unnecessary personal "I" agendas.

PRACTICE: What Do I Need?

Right now, what do you need? Your mind can provide a wish list—don't go there. You don't need those things. Right now, again, what do you need? Settle into your body, drop down from your thinking processes, and ask *what do I need, right now?* Continue repeating the same question until the truth arises. You don't need anything at all.

Self-acceptance isn't passive. It doesn't mean that you will cease personal development and inner growth. Rather, it offers the capacity to adapt and change behaviors with increased ease. With acceptance comes the knowing that your personality will change as you mature. The return on inner growth and self-reflection benefits your personality. Remain open to modifying and adapting to life as you go. Personal growth through investigation becomes an ongoing practice as your self-awareness increases. Your motivation to grow comes from an organic, evolutionary aspect of being human.

With self-acceptance there is no pressure to be other than who you are. You can be responsible for your own growth. Access feedback from others, adopt what is useful to you and dismiss the rest. Self-acceptance prepares you to change with ease. You won't take on others' advice or criticism because of who they are. With objectivity (impersonal lens of perception) criticism is useful or it's not. Either way, it presents no threat.

PRACTICE: The Feeling of Self-Acceptance

Read through this exercise first. Then close your eyes, sense the spaciousness, and watch the feather. Let's get out of your head by relaxing your shoulders and your belly. Close your eyes. Drop your energy from your head to your torso and imagine that inside your body there is an open space. Take a moment and sense spaciousness within you. Imagine a pillow feather falling from the top of your head down through your neck, into the inner spaciousness. Watch it as it slowly drops down to your pelvis. Don't rush it. Don't make it do anything. It might drift from side to side as it descends. When the feather lands, continue watching it for a few moments. Rest within your torso, in the internal spaciousness. It's a zone where you can sense that everything is okay. Let the feeling of self-acceptance arise. It is naturally accessible in the absence of self-rejection.

CHAPTER 25

Attention

How do you use your attention? When you are speaking with somebody and you have lost interest in what they are saying, do you pay more attention to your self-talk than to what they have to say? Does your attention rest on privately held opinions like *I wish they'd just stop talking*, or *How can I get away from this person?* If you are speaking with somebody to whom you are sexually attracted, does your self-referencing chatter include *Do I have a chance here?* or *Can they pick up that I think they are cute?* Do you monitor someone's approval of you while you are talking to them? What about when they are someone in authority? In each case, how much attention is given to the task you are outwardly doing, and how much is supporting your inner mind chatter?

Think of your span of attention as having a particular bandwidth. When some of your attention is entertaining your internal dialogue, you have less bandwidth to pay attention to what is happening in that moment. You are not fully present. You have compromised your attention, entertaining both what's happening in the present, and self-talk. The DMN readily consumes as much bandwidth as it can command because its job is to keep the idea of a personal "you" active. How much of your bandwidth is deviated to self-talk while you are communicating face-to-face with other people? Start watching so that you can become aware of your own habits.

It's common that one forgets about one's inner spiritual nature during a regular busy day. The real issue is that one's bandwidth of attention is already split between self-talk and external events. The natural way to honor our divinity and our humanity is to reroute attention from self-talk to our inner spiritual nature. You can withdraw your extra bandwidth from self-referencing stories and use it to access the inner realm of consciousness. The extra bandwidth is our capacity for internal stillness in spite of external circumstances. How to do this? It's easier than one can imagine.

When one is spiritually awake, the extra bandwidth of attention is at home within, in silence. There is no interest in adhering attention to the DMN. It has nothing to offer but lies. The energy loss of that bad habit is seen through, and attention rests at home. Peace, calm, and well-being are the natural, internal anchors.

On my own journey, I can remember recognizing that self-referencing was happening while I was in conversation with others. My first approach was to place all my attention on what was taking place around me, in front of me. In doing so I paid no attention to self-talk. I learned what it meant to be fully present. Within a few days of this practice during every communication I felt I was placing too much attention to events in the external world. I felt physically disoriented and out of balance. I needed to keep something inside. I recognized that my full bandwidth of attention wasn't needed in order to be fully present in conversation, yet I also needed to stop entertaining self-talk. I had the idea that perhaps the capacity formerly dedicated to self-talk could be allocated to being aware of the still, spaciousness within. I felt as though I was unplugging a power supply from my self-referential narrative and engaging it in my torso. I was shifting extra bandwidth of attention to inner stillness. In hindsight, I took a circuitous route by engaging all of my attention outwardly. Going outward to come back inward is not necessary.

The efficient route is to first be aware of your attention resting within. Drop in or zoom back out, whichever direction works best for you. Keep about ten percent of your bandwidth of attention within, resting on your spiritual nature, and use the bulk of your attention doing whatever it is you need to do. Start from within and retain some attention at home. Be present to whatever requires your attention. Your bandwidth cannot stretch from self-referencing to inner stillness.

When we self-reference we abandon inner stillness. Choose inner stillness and there will be less attention allocated to self-referencing.

Post-awakening, my experience is different. Attention rests within, sometimes all of it, sometimes part of it. I never seem to forget it. I find it very useful when my husband asks, "what are you thinking about?" I can check to see where my attention is. Sometimes I'm thinking about things, processing or planning, and other times there is nothing going on in my head at all. If I notice I am revisiting a conversation that has already happened, then there is something to be learned. Revisiting conversations that are in the past, or rerunning different versions of conversations, is invariably a symptom of some discomfort in my personality. It is a call to investigation because my personality needs some attention and something new needs to be seen. All the while, attention never fully leaves my spiritual nature; it is anchored there within, and so far seems solid as a rock.

PRACTICE: Attention

Be fully present with whatever is happening. Stop listening to your thoughts and be present. Place your attention within your torso and close your eyes. Tune into the sense of knowingness that is always within you. Rest there for a few minutes until self-talk settles down. Keep about ten percent of your attention within and open your eyes. Let seeing happen and keep some attention within. Engage your senses. What do you see? What do you hear? Your mind can label and identify what is seen and heard, and all the while retain ten percent of your attention within. This practice is invaluable for training your attention to rest in your spiritual nature and be present to the world at the same time. What's the price? There is no attention remaining to support a belief in the self-referencing network.

CHAPTER 26

Neither Special nor Unworthy

Believing you are unworthy comes with a need to feel special. We are usually aware of one more than the other, yet both habits must be identified to whatever degree they are present in us. Then they can be dropped together. The experience of specialness is transient—once the experience passes it is replaced with the feeling of lack. The feeling of lack lasts much longer than the feeling of thinking you are special. There is no winning in this mind game. There is nothing to be gained from either; together they support a conditioned false identity.

Your spiritual nature is neither enough, lacking, unworthy, nor special. People who are spiritually free know that being fully divine while having a human experience requires recognizing and acknowledging their ordinariness. Being ordinary means dropping the need to be seen in a particular way. Others are free to perceive as they do. Without acceptance of ordinariness there is a propensity for pretense and a motivation to seek attention. There is no freedom in that. There is freedom in embracing ordinariness.

Thomas believed he was special. His mother repeatedly told him so in his childhood. He spent 30 years of adulthood trying to prove his specialness to himself and those around him. I asked him, "what's wrong with being ordinary?" To him, ordinariness meant failure, a mundane existence, letting both himself and his mother down badly. Could he have misinterpreted his mother's message? Maybe she was doing her best to instill confidence in him, trying to give him something better than what she had been told. Maybe what she really told him was another version of whatever she heard in her childhood. I asked him to let himself off the hook with his mother's story and to end his obligation to be special. It is time to reclaim his authority and to live his own life. He felt a huge relief and broke down. He spoke about his deep-seated sense of unworthiness because he couldn't attain an acceptable standard of specialness in his own eyes. No matter what he achieved in his life, he continued to raise the standard of what it took to be and feel special. Ordinariness isn't failure; it is self-acceptance that comes from honoring what is natural to us.

Do you want to feel special? Do you want your offerings to be acknowledged and recognized by others? Underpinning the desire to be special is a fallacy about your true identity: who I am is how I am perceived. Stop believing that how you are seen is of value to you. It's not important unless you make it so.

Jenny told me that feeling unworthy was a familiar feeling. She yearned to feel special, but it almost never happened because of her attachment to unworthiness. Her way out, once she saw the double-sided pattern, included cultivating self-love and ending her self-judging commentary in her mind. Her relationship with herself needed to include tenderness and acceptance to replace self-indulgent self-pity. As she worked on changing her internal landscape, she came to recognize that being ordinary gave her a sense of connection with others. She saw herself as an equal for the first time. Being ordinary opened her up to a unified viewpoint. Her lens of perception that created separation was held together by her belief in her own unworthiness. She now had distance from the personal identity. Ordinariness was her ticket to abandon the "me" story. In its absence she had access to the unified lens of perception where we naturally pay attention to what is the same, first, and where diversity is perceived only to help us to function.

PRACTICE: Be Ordinary

Spend one week reminding yourself that you are ordinary. Take it on as a spiritual practice for seven days. Anything less won't crack this one. Repeat the sentence "I'm an ordinary person living an ordinary life" as often as you can remember over the week. Notice any resistance that arises when you say the sentence. Don't engage in the story content of resistance. Without an emotional reaction (resistance) the authentic acceptance of the ordinariness of being human can settle in. See if you can let yourself off the hook, no longer playing the games to secure your identity from how others perceive you. Be ordinary; it's underrated.

PART 6

BRING IT ON!

CHAPTER 27

Authentic Contentment

Contentment is often misunderstood. We make the error of believing that contentment is the consequence of getting what we want. If we want something—reaching a goal, finishing a task, having sex or a piece of chocolate—and we get that thing, we imagine that the contentment we feel is because we got what we wanted. In this we are mistaken. Contentment isn't a consequence. The capacity to feel contentment is within us all the time. When our attention is directed toward wanting something, that thing becomes our focus. Then we get it. The wanting stops, and our attention comes to rest. We call it "contentment," and attribute contentment to the things we got. Contentment, however, is actually a natural baseline feeling independent to wanting anything. If the only time we don't want something is after we get something, then we are in the pause space between two desires. One has subsided and the next hasn't cranked up yet. We feel content because our attention is now available; it's not caught up in wanting. Take external factors out of it. Feeling content is your innate capacity. Don't attribute the feeling to objects and circumstances. Practice feeling content.

You may be thinking, *does this mean I can't enjoy things?* You can enjoy things and also not miss them when they're not around. Because "things" aren't the source of contentment. There is contentment, and things are enjoyed. We are no longer giving things potency and value beyond what they can offer. *I'm OK just as I am?* Yes. You are.

You don't need any reason to be content. Attention is withdrawn from the story making self-referencing network. Ideas that draw on the past or the future are not entertained. Contentment is an internal state that you can experience right now. It brings calmness and a break from your thoughts. Being content is a decision. Contentment is in this present moment, if you choose to experience it.

PRACTICE: Be Content

Make the decision to be content. Right now, feel contentment. When resistance arises don't believe the rhetoric; instead say, "I see through you" and be content. Peace and calm will arise; rest in it. Contentment cultivates acceptance of life as it is.

CHAPTER 28

Break the Rules

Do you give yourself a lot of orders, instructions, and recommendations? Do you give yourself a hard time? Do you have high expectations for yourself? Are you frequently commenting to yourself that you should do this or that? Have you established rules of what you should and should not do, how you should and should not behave, feel, or look? In short, do you *should* yourself?

When we should ourselves, we are placing rules on ourselves. What if we dropped these limiting thoughts? Shoulds are established by the mind to create what we believe is a better version of "me." We know that how we behave is not what stops us from being free; believing the mind is. Self-talk that emphasizes shoulds, rules, and obligations has content that is difficult to ignore. It's invariably supported by a belief that our shoulds are a necessary control mechanism keeping us safe. This thinking can be indicative of trauma held in the body, and unresolved trauma makes us should ourselves. Know that your shoulds don't keep you safe; they are a learned habit, scars from trying to control what we think we can't control. Shoulds have no inherent value.

If you are someone who tries to be good, or if you have personal rules and shoulds that guide your way on, it's time to call your own bluff. See what happens if you break your own rules, if you consciously do what you should not do. Pushing against your shoulds involves boldly disobeying your own rules, defying the dictates of your own mind. Experience what happens if you don't obey your own rules. Test your own belief system and find out if the consequences resemble what you thought they might be. This practice is fun. Break your own rules.

Breaking your own rules throws you into new experiences. The added advantage of new experiences is that they provide a workout for your brain, creating new neural pathways. Having new experiences is one of the best things you can do for your mental health.

PRACTICE: I'd Never Wear That

Go to charity clothing stores and buy obscure garments. Choose colors that don't work together and styles that clash. Change your style of dress for three weeks and monitor your mind closely as you go to familiar places wearing outfits that you think you should be paid to wear in public. Let your self-image take a hit and see what comes up for you. Don't make excuses, go about your business as normal.

Changing your self-image in this way, for three weeks, could mean that you dress inappropriately for your age, gender, or sexual orientation. You might choose to dress in a style stereotypical of folks you would not normally hang out with. This challenges how you see yourself and how you want to be seen. You can be self-conscious or embarrassed in your new gear, or you can create new neural pathways and be relaxed and confident in your new attire. Can you stay in the present and not run self-referencing stories about how you are possibly being perceived?

PRACTICE: Step Out of the Box

Make a list of five things that you would never do. You might have to complete all items on your list, though usually two or three items will suffice. Each time you stretch outside of your comfort zone, observe your mind closely. Two more items to add to your list are:

1. Give away a large sum of money (an obscene amount is even better if you can afford it) to a random busker or street entertainer. Watch what your mind does before, during, and after your gesture of kindness.

2. If you think you can't sing or you are too embarrassed to do so in public, go to a karaoke and perform two songs with confidence, fully sober. Stay present, on task, and don't believe your thoughts.

The goals in these exercises is to dismantle your own resistance and stop entertaining your inner strategy for self-punishment. If you are an anxious person, go gently with this exercise. Take it slowly. Start with baby steps—your attachment to control is stronger than most.

Spiritual practices that can shake up deeply rooted thinking patterns must be approached with maturity. This work does not give you a free pass to be a horrible person. The purpose is to learn to be fully responsible for your inner reality: your thoughts and emotions. Outward behavior is the trigger for you to see your inner reality so that you then see through the rules imposed by your mind.

CHAPTER 29

Surrender

I made many decisions in the name of my spiritual search that were described as drastic and unnecessary by my friends and family. Without support, I left my marriage, knew I would never have children, and walked away from a successful career. I left Ireland with a rucksack on my back knowing that if I were to truly abandon my values, my beliefs, and my ideas of who I was, I would have to abandon my life as I had created and known it.

I first went to a campsite in the south of Spain and spent the next three months watching my thoughts and engaging in spiritual practices. I worked with forgiveness—forgiving others and myself. I made a list of fears and worked to separate the emotion of fear from my memories. I had a fear of horses from negative experiences during childhood, so I found a horse riding school and had some lessons until I learned how to relate to horses without fear. I made a bucket list and investigated each item whittling it down to the things I believed that I needed to do in order to honor my own life. I gained new insights into the workings of my mind, which is inevitable when there is nothing to distract one from the exercise. Two years later, a new home base showed up in India. I had dedicated my life to the spiritual path, to always working on a specific focus, to breaking old habits, to dropping beliefs, and to strengthening my ability to focus my attention within.

I once dedicated many weeks to listening within, and following only the inner impetus to move, to speak, and to take action. I made the conscious decision not to obey directives that originated from conceptual thought processing. My time was spent being aware of stillness within and listening rather than doing and thinking. Mornings were dictated by physical needs; my body was taking care of itself. Then I would sit and simply be, attentive only to inner stillness. I had given myself a chance to slow down to the point of being able to recognize the source of every action. Was my mind motivating every action, or was there another impetus influencing me? I noticed that an inner directive to take action moved my body first, and seconds later my mind responded with skills to facilitate the doing of tasks. Without deciding what to do, my mind would listen and play catch up with what was already in motion. My mind was serving and supporting what began deeper within. I noticed that my body honored the deeper impetus and I would eat, read, walk, and occasionally hang out in a chai shop—all prompted from the stillness of true spiritual nature within. My routine changed. I would bathe at unpredictable times of the day. Not everything I did seemed efficient. I remember buying newspapers which I didn't read. I continued listening within.

Ideas like *I want a cup of coffee* fell away as easily as they arose. There wasn't enough attention given to any idea to shift it from thought to action; it was the other way around. Action would begin, and my mind would play catch-up. Another motivator was directing me. I was responding. Self-serving ideas no longer had potency. When desires such as wanting to watch a movie arose in my mind, the idea would soon drop because my interest in supporting mind-created intentions faded out. Yet, at other times, it happened that my body turned on my computer and a movie was watched. It became increasingly clear what ideas were supporting the "me" and, in contrast, how it now felt to have a deeper inner capacity guiding my way. During those weeks, whenever my attention went to thoughts such as *I'm bored* or *I want a distraction*, I would say *I see through you* to my mind and return my attention to inner rest. I saw that my attention was at rest unless it was attracted by thought or an external distraction. It wasn't and isn't an effort to have my attention rest within; that's its natural place. I was learning how to be. Action was taking place, and the personal perspective wasn't initiating, doing, nor owning it. The absence of the personal lens of perception allowed my heart to further open. Thoughts showed up in stark contrast to the inner stillness. My thoughts were repetitious, each presenting some idea that would make things better. The truth was that nothing needed to be better until my mind said so. Exquisite inner calm, peace, and love were the experience in the absence of thoughts.

The difference in tone, content, and quality between the directives with a personal agenda and the flow that came from within (deeper than thought) became pronounced. My mind was following, not controlling. There was implicit trust because I wasn't informed about what was going on prior to my participation in an action. My actions were in the present, and my body played its part. My mind was no longer interpreting each scene to help decipher my next or best move. I understood that there is an innate impetus within each of us to move, engage, and participate in life. Call it "awareness," "life force," "divinity," "vitality," or a "universal flow"— it moves all of creation, each species, both fauna and flora, according to its own inner nature. Our minds think we know better, that we can improve on the flow of life itself. I found out that this is not true. All we need to do is get out of our own way.

PRACTICE: Catch-Up

Schedule about half of a day for this exercise. From the moment you awaken, don't do anything; don't even move. Listen inwardly. Wait until something deeper stirs you forward. Don't follow your ideas about what to do or what needs to be done. Don't crank up your thoughts about the day ahead. Rest within. Watch to see what unfolds. If your thoughts meander, pull your attention inward without judgment. The first move will be your body needing to use a bathroom. Your body will tell you when that is. Afterwards rest and listen to see what happens next. If you are standing in your bathroom for an hour then be with that. The task is to be ok with whatever is happening. There is no right or wrong. You are either listening and responding, or you are directed by your mind. Be moved from something deeper than mind.

Whom do you serve? You cannot serve both your inner urge and your thoughts. For as long as your self-referencing network guides your way, you will remain in the prison of your own thoughts. It is a leap of faith to trust your inner knowing to guide your way; surrendering is required.

PRACTICE: Surrender

Listen to the sound of inner silence. Drop all stories and listen to silence. Drop deeper within (or zoom out). Don't do anything until you are stirred from what is deeper than your mind. Wait. Stop everything. Let something else make the next move. Let your role in this moment and the next be directed from within, by that which is pure and wiser than your personal viewpoint. Be honest with yourself: Can you let go of the habitual idea that your thoughts are in control? Will you surrender?

Both of these exercises stir the personal belief that we are in control. Can you surrender and allow? You'll find that not only are you stepping out of the way but also that "you" are absent when your attention is aligned with silence and rest within. Are you ready to surrender the self-serving tricks of the personal agenda? Will you let another, greater order have its way with you? Can you let it dismantle you? And reassemble you? True surrender is when we recognize that we were never in control. Our minds create the ideas that we initiate and own our action. The personal viewpoint was never the one initiating action; your "me" construct was an overlay that distracted you from the potency of what was in charge all along. Your spiritual nature, pure consciousness is doing everything, all of it.

CHAPTER 30

Meditate and Investigate

Not everyone can leave their established life in pursuit of spirituality. While this was my path, it's not necessary to do so. Life itself is a spiritual practice, no matter where it happens or how it unfolds. It's a question of orienting our viewpoint so that we can observe normal everyday events as opportunities to notice how our minds can play us. In this chapter we explore how meditative practices (using mindfulness as an example) can help improve our daily experience of living and propel us towards fearless freedom. We will also apply our understanding of how the brain works, in order to get more benefit from any meditation practice.

Meditation techniques (new and traditional) are growing in popularity, perhaps most noticeably, mindfulness. Mindfulness is a practice that helps us become present, open, and available to life. The practice itself is simple: acknowledge your thoughts, and do not engage in their content. The mindfulness perspective is a place you look *from*. The act of being mindful causes a shift in your perspective toward increased objectivity and detachment. As thoughts come and go, you recognize them as thoughts first and foremost; their story content is secondary.

What if thoughts reemerge (as they inevitably do)? When this happens, your job is to see your thoughts without engaging in their story. When your attention is available to be present, you are not reacting from memory. There is little else to do in the practice itself. The place you are looking from, the mindfulness viewpoint is peaceful, open in the absence of contraction.

Mindfulness offers a simple and effective method to be in a relationship with your thoughts and with your life. It is relatively easy and accessible, requiring an unintimidating amount of effort. The practice helps you to become familiar with *being*, as opposed to *doing*. Inner stillness is indirectly cultivated. It is a good antidote to stress and anxiety by bringing physiological ease to your nervous system and by cultivating healthy neural habits. However, many who practice mindfulness have told me that in spite of their working familiarity with it, they continue to experience emotional volatility in their personal lives. "I've practiced mindfulness for fifteen years and I'm still emotionally sensitive, insecure, and live with a deep-rooted anxiety about the future," they might say. Or, "I teach mindfulness, but my own life is a mess." These experiences are not uncommon.

It's imperative to consciously recognize when you are slipping out of objectivity and sliding towards the content of your thoughts. Being present and operating from your story cannot happen at the same time, though your mind can convince you otherwise. On a day that begins with a mindfulness meditation, how long do you continue to enjoy the centeredness and objectivity that the practice can bring? Do you notice when the inner calmness begins to peter out? Are you lost in the story of your life long before you are cognizant of the shift away from inner awareness? When you can see the story-making mechanism of your mind from the mindfulness viewing point, there is internal peace and it emanates from you to others. You are fully present. When the mindfulness perspective is abandoned, and engagement with thoughts has bound you to a subjective reality, it is inevitable that the state of inner equanimity disappears.

PRACTICE: Identification and Investigation

The next time you have a good meditation pay attention to the next phenomenal experience, mind story, or emotion that grabs your attention. Identify what it is that shifts you out of your meditative state. What is the event or story or emotion that commands all of your attention? Your answer to this question requires investigation. Spiritual progress does not advance our human psychology; our psychology inhibits our progress inevitably at some point along the path. Identify what brings the "me," the personal lens of perception, back into focus. Then investigate so you can find out why. Why does that circumstance/ thought catch your attention and create the contracted state of the personal again? Through investigation you can break the potency of the pattern by bringing underpinning beliefs and values into your awareness with objectivity.

CHAPTER 31

Mindfulness and Brain Rewiring

You do not need a calm life that is free of responsibilities in order to remain mindful. You are invited to trust that without a personal subjective story guiding your way, you can function well and respond to what life presents. A practice to train your brain to function differently to its habitual pattern will create a substantial shift in how you function. Spiritual practice that requires your body to be still trains your brain to associate physical stillness with not using your self-referencing network. If the only time you consciously disconnect from believing personal thoughts is when you are sitting still in meditation, then your brain will always require this condition in order to disengage from your self-referencing network. Yet most actions are more efficiently managed by your task-oriented network, without interference from the self-referencing mechanism.

Learning how to use your TON without the DMN is what enables you to engage your life with continued awareness, stillness, and peace. Traditional spiritual practices encourage disconnection from the DMN by bringing awareness to its strongest neural pathways. Useful tools that prune the DMN include recognizing that we are not the doer of any action, which takes personal ownership out of the equation. Having no attachment to outcomes drops the personal agenda. Ceasing judgments of others lessens the belief in separation. When we use these tools, we are pruning the DMN one neural pathway at a time. Useful as these tools are, I have found they are not enough to create the shifts in perspective needed for spiritual freedom. Fearless freedom is experienced when you are motivated only to follow through on the direct movement from the inner stillness. To be led by the thinking, subjective mind is imprisonment. If you don't tackle the overlap between your DMN and your TON, your DMN will be eager to claim ownership, recognition, and attention. It will be invested in outcomes and convince you that it needs to be in control.

How you operate within any given day will change, and that is what brings a qualitative difference to how you experience your life. You do not need to be seated or confined to a space of silence with your eyes closed to shift your perspective to the mindfulness viewpoint. The perspective is not limited to a meditative practice.

Below are three practical tips to help retrain your brain. They are incremental and should be mastered sequentially.

PRACTICE: Mindfulness and Movement

Relax your body. Be present by paying attention only to your senses for a minute or two. Close your eyes. Now go deeper and be aware of inner stillness. Inhabit the stillness. Be the stillness. After a couple of minutes, move your body and do not leave your internal viewing point. Remain merged with inner stillness. Lift your arms over your head. Next stretch out your arms to the sides and in front of you. Remain within while there is also a subtle awareness of your arms extending.

PRACTICE: Mindfulness and Vision

If you can do the first exercise without being distracted by any story, open your eyes and look around. Let seeing happen. Don't run the story. Don't say, "I am looking at this or that." Nobody is looking at anything unless you engage your mind to run that story. Let there be the activity of looking only. It should feel the same within you whether your eyes are open or closed. If your attention is more outwardly focused when you open your eyes, know that the activation of your vision is automatically activating your self-referencing network. Whatever level of stillness you are aware of within you, it need not change whether your eyes are open or closed.

PRACTICE: Mindfulness and Action

Select an activity that does not require your full concentration. Identify an activity you can perform and still retain a capacity to be relaxed and aware, noticing thoughts but not engaging in their content. For example, you may try cooking, driving a familiar route, cleaning, taking a shower, or exercising.

Pay close attention as you undertake one or more of these familiar tasks. Notice whether your mind drifts into personal stories. Do you talk to yourself internally or perhaps audibly? While your TON is working, be mindful, don't engage your self-referencing network while doing tasks. By being mindful you are withdrawing your extra bandwidth of attention within. Your TON operates better without self-referential interference. Let tasks happen without "me."

Make a list of the daily activities that you know can be performed as a moving meditation. The attention formerly allocated to your DMN will become available within. It will be as though you are aware of the screen on which a movie is being played while you are watching the movie. As you learn to use the TON without reliance on the DMN life will appear to get smoother; it flows more organically. This is a consequence of disengaging from the DMN's viewpoint. Planning to make this shift in how your brain works is quite different than engaging in the practice; take both steps. Put in the effort to make this internal change manifest positive results. Recognize the thoughts that present obstacles; they are only thoughts. Ignore the unsupportive internal narrative that wants to avoid change. Take the step and make these changes to your day, every day.

When you lose contact with inner awareness while talking and engaging with others, a wonderful opportunity arises. You have identified that your DMN is filtering communication. Take note of the conversations, topics and people that draw you into your personal perspective. Nobody has the power to lure your attention from objectivity to subjectivity. Abiding in your spiritual nature requires a change in how your brain works. The good news is that changing how your brain works, undoing your conditioned neural pathways, is truly not that difficult as long as you are willing to let go of identifying with your conditioning.

You can change how your brain works; go for it! If you discover that conversation cannot happen without shifting your viewpoint from inner awareness to personal perspective, then practice the first two exercises to help free your TON from your DMN. Your goal is to be able to take action with ease while remaining experientially in touch with inner stillness.

PRACTICE: Mindfulness and Conversation

Go to the grocery store or a coffee shop by yourself. Drop in and touch into your spiritual nature. Have brief functional conversations with serving staff in each establishment. Short habitual dialogues are exchanges that you can engage while your attention is consciously not running a personal, opinionated commentary. Make sure your attention is in touch with an inner experience of spaciousness or stillness while you speak.

Slowly build a circle of people that you can communicate with without running a personal, self-referencing story. Success comes when you are available to be present in your communication with others; your attention doesn't stray to internal commentary. Loved ones will present your biggest tests. Without internal commentary there will be no habitual emotional reactions. You won't be operating from memory. There will be a constant awareness of a wider spacious viewpoint within you as you interact with others and go about your daily activities.

PART 7

BURSTING THE SPIRITUAL BUBBLE

CHAPTER 32

Call off the Search

What motivates your spiritual search? Is it motivated by a personal perspective that seeks a better, happier life? Or is it motivated by an urge from the divine essence within you that is deeper than thought? In the case of the latter, you innately know that you are not able to permanently stop your spiritual search no matter how much you want to cast it aside. Spiritual maturation has its own momentum because some other force, deeper than personal motivation, is in charge of navigation.

After you finish this book, make a decision to drop your spiritual search for a specified period of time. It's important that you decide how long the break period should last so that you can review and learn from the exercise. You might allocate four weeks, two months, or an entire year. Choose a period of time that is just outside your comfort zone. Once you decide, mark the end date in your calendar. After that date you will either have embarked on another, more interesting project that piqued your interest, or you will resume your journey. Either way maturation will have taken place.

Notice what the suggestion of this exercise brings up for you. Clear your mind chatter and any emotional reactions—you have the tools to do so from earlier chapters in this book. The purpose of this exercise is twofold. First it will clear any attachment that you might have to the story of your journey and to being a seeker. Second, and more importantly, you will find out whether your motivation to awaken is rooted in a personal agenda, or whether there is an authentic inner yearning that signifies it's your time to awaken, abide, and live in the truth that lies deeper than thought. Put it another way, *Is your spiritual journey guided by your divine essence or a personal agenda?* If the latter, you will find another hobby that offers fun and distraction during the pause period. If your spiritual path is an authentic call to freedom, you will not be able to totally halt your spiritual endeavors. The work that is the hallmark of a spiritual path, such as tidying up your thinking patterns and observing thoughts, will continue within you even if you refuse to read a line of spiritual text or consciously participate in any spiritual practice. The inner divine essence will insist on having its way with you, no matter how much you try to ignore it because something deeper than thought is sitting in the driver's seat of your life.

If you discover that your interest in spirituality has faded and your life has oriented in a new direction, honor that path. Spirituality isn't going to give you a nicer life, so if you find yourself wanting to take a different path, take the brave step to follow it. Be honest with yourself, and give yourself the experiences that you need, not what your mind thinks you need. After your pause period your mind will no longer be entangled with your spiritual search. You will know that seeking happens on its own. Seeking has its own momentum, and your personal agenda is no longer involved; you have stepped out of the way. You are listening, not directing. You can understand how thoughts may have at one stage hijacked the pursuit of their own absence.

CHAPTER 33

Original Identity

Recognizing the truth of who you are is the ultimate teaching of many spiritual traditions. The terms "enlightenment," "abiding awakening," and "self-realization" are the most commonly used terms to mark internal recognition of your spiritual nature together with the cessation of self-referencing of perceptions.

Get to know your original identity by spending time resting within. Abide in what is spontaneously present without having to be thought. Notice when abiding happens of its own accord during the day. Does it happen in the shower or when you are driving and alone in your vehicle? Does it happen when you exercise or spend time in nature? Notice when there is inner stillness and rest within—a state that isn't created by your thinking.

Notice when there is a gap in your personal experience of existence, when there is no "me." At first you will notice it only when the "me" returns, indicated by the shift to the contracted viewpoint of the personal. When you shift from false identity created by mind to your original identity, add the concept *that is what/who I really am*. This shift in identity considerably weakens your intention to support thoughts generated by your self-referencing network. It will soon be too much effort to support a false self-image and persona. Your original identity is at rest, rich and complete, no matter what events are happening in life.

Peace and truth are found in the absence of the false. As soon as your attention goes back into your thoughts, doubts will arise and sabotage your experience and inner knowing with judgments. Your mind is your survival mechanism for coping in the external world. It tries to assess and control. It tries to monitor the value and efficacy of the peace and rest that lies deeper than thought. It will make a story out of an inner experience which has no story. Our minds can try to make everything better for "me." The mind can believe we will be better off once we are awake or free. Spirituality doesn't work in that way. It's in the absence of such beliefs that we find freedom. Spirituality is the process of returning home, remembering who you knew yourself to be before you believed your thoughts. Spirituality helps you to understand how your neural pathways created a mistaken identity.

It would be remiss of me to imply that recognizing your true nature is the end of your spiritual journey. If it is in your destiny to go further than awakening, the post-awakening journey will begin when the concept of identity is exposed to be nothing other than another thought, believed to have meaning and significance. Both who you previously believed yourself to be and the recognition of your true self rest on a need for identity. Identity is a concept, and it too falls away. Exploring the steps from awakening to liberation is beyond the scope of this book. It's in my nature however to crack the glass ceiling of awakening and shine a light on vistas that lie beyond. For now, get solid in the recognition of your true nature—that which is not a product of conditioned thinking. Allowing ample time to learn how to function in your life without self-referencing will establish a solid foundation from which you can leap beyond all identity.

CHAPTER 34

Fear of Absence

Are you afraid of losing your health, your vitality, or your life force? Are you afraid of being without love, people, animals, food, shelter, and money? Are you uneasy, knowing that whatever you value can be taken from you faster than it was given to you? That your body will die, and your stories will fade in time—ultimately to be forgotten?

If you are experiencing an emotional reaction to any of these questions, there is work to do in order to dissolve your attachments to your preferences and desires for something other than what is inevitable. The idea of death and our subsequent absence cause difficulty for us only when we are alive. The reason we fear death when we are alive is because we fear what we can't control. After your body has died, you won't have a problem with death or how it happened. You survived the transition into your body, and you will manage the exit also and none of this will matter to you after you cease to physically exist.

In many cultures we are uncomfortable with death, even though none of us can escape it. If we prepare for our own death, we can unearth some hidden fears which can help us grow spiritually. It's a fruitful exercise practically, too, assisting those who survive us to close out our lives.

If you haven't done so already, take steps to prepare for your physical death. Write your last will and testament. Decide what should happen to your body. Make a list of bank accounts and other details that will help others tidy up and close your life. Tell someone close to you where you have placed your closing documents. Taking these steps will help to accept physical death. It invites you to think about life going on in your absence. It brings the reality of your death front and central.

Awakening brings on another kind of death, one that is unique to the spiritual path. Who you believe yourself to be must die for you to abide in an awakened state. Your body remains alive while you no longer identify as being the personality that your brain constructs and maintains. Death of the idea of "me" is only a problem for "me." Just as fear of physical death is an idea entertained when you are alive and has no significance after your death, the fear of "me" disappearing has no potency post awakening. Your physical absence is inevitable with death and awakening changes the function of your personality. You cannot control either. You can however envisage the outcome of both and be more at ease by accepting what's inevitable. If these words trigger an emotional reaction, bring your attention into your body and be gentle with yourself. Move towards a loving, open acceptance of death.

If you are fearful of your own absence it is because an emotion is linked to a thought in your mind. Drop in to your true nature and observe that a thought is separate from an emotion. Decouple fear from the thought of death. An attitude of ease, relief, closure, and rest can replace emotions of fear and anxiety. Work towards an authentic acceptance of your physical death and welcome the death of "me"— the one who you believe yourself to be.

PRACTICE: Break the Habit of Being Fearful

The sequence from a believed thought to emotional reaction can be broken, freeing you from habitual fear. First you will need to recognize the sequence. How? By being willing to be objective and having the courage to change your relationship with fear.

1. Bring to mind one thing that triggers fear for you.

2. See that it is the thought of that thing that creates fear, not the thing itself.

3. Take a moment to recognize that the origin of fear is in your mind.

Fear happens when a thought that is believed to be true triggers an emotional reaction. Separate the thought from your emotions by not having an emotional reaction. How? By allowing the thought to be in your mind while you breathe calmness into your body. Guide your body into the rest and digest state. Spend some time on this; you are creating new neural pathways allowing certain thoughts to be in mind without automatically co-opting emotions. You are breaking the habitual sequence between thoughts and emotions.

CHAPTER 35

Stay the Course

There were a couple of phases during my own journey where my mind kicked back. It was no longer willing to run with the program of spiritual awakening. Habitual beliefs, attitudes, opinions, and judgments would come together and sabotage my progress. My mind would hold fast to the viewpoint that spirituality was full of concepts and that "me" stories and personal life events were authentic. It was as though spiritual reality and thought-created reality were competing for my attention and validation. I questioned my spiritual insights and experiences, thinking, *perhaps I was brainwashed and imagined my openings.* Suffering had an undeniable authentic reality about it. *Surely, I should trust that more than spiritual experiences,* I thought.

These phases were difficult. My thinking process would negate clarity and the inner knowing of pure consciousness, reducing any spiritual attainment to concepts and memory. Personal drama seemed more convincing. How could pure consciousness be real? Surely the intensity of suffering was real, and spirituality was make-believe, created by my imagination. This one way is how attachment to the personal story played out for me.

What helped me through these times was picturing someone whom I believed was a great spiritual teacher. I would address them in my mind: *I know you know something that I don't know. You lived from a viewpoint that I have no access to right now. I have to trust that I'm the one who is deluded and that you are far beyond where I am at today, even though logic tells me you could have been delusional. I have to trust that you know more and can see a bigger picture.* I needed faith. Sometimes I pleaded to be dragged from my despair—thinking *pull me to where you are looking from*—when suffering was too intense to bear. During these phases my breathing was shallow; I couldn't sleep; I could find no way out. Spiritual practices and techniques were futile. All I could do was have patience and faith while I waited for it to pass. I had to wait for the experience of being lost to the play of mind to run its course and in the meantime hold fast in faith to those who walked the path before me.

Desperate for a story, the mind will find evidence to support its claims that the personal is real and that pure consciousness is an imagined utopia—that you are fooling yourself all along your spiritual path. Doubt will arise. This is the time to stay the course and to stop protecting the personal viewpoint.

Surround yourself with those who have walked the path before you. Have faith in the wisdom of spiritual teachings and books if a deeper, internal knowing resonates with them. What you cannot access during times of spiritual despair is held in faith until you can walk in freedom.

CHAPTER 36

Imperfection

I've never felt the need to be perfect in order to love myself. Loving my imperfection is easier and more natural for me. Online slogans with sentiments like "you are perfect just as you are" confuse me. Why would I want or need to be perfect? Where's the growth in that? Perhaps the idea is that imperfection is perfect. Imperfection to me is natural, authentic, and integral to being human.

There seems to be a myth that some human beings are perfect. Perhaps we want to believe this is true in order to deify our role models, our leaders, and our teachers. We can with some imagination assume they have perfect health, behavior, feelings, and intellect. We can decide that they are perfect in every respect, but that's not true. When we project perfection onto another, we are being naïve. We are denying their humanity, and we are judging ours. We edit our perception and see what we want to see. In ignorance, we look outward for perfection as though perfection is a goal.

All people by virtue of being human are imperfect. The constant and infinite cycle of human evolution has inbuilt imperfection. Without it, growth and change cannot happen. Evolution does not aim for perfection; it is not garnering direction from lofty ideals that mark the ultimate perfect human. When we recognize that imperfection is a natural attribute of humanity, an objective attitude and transparency toward our own human imperfection unfolds.

There is a natural impetus in each of us to continue to evolve throughout our lives. Discover your innate motivation to create better versions of yourself as you grow older, not in rejection of who you currently are, but for the innate draw toward growth and learning.

Ongoing evolution is about the journey, not the destination. Without our imperfections we become stagnant and unhealthy in mind and body. The natural order is that imperfection motivates a healthy interest in personal growth and lifelong learning. If you habitually see human imperfection in a judgmental way, break the habit with new understanding and perspectives.

Be open and objective when you perceive people you admire. Engage your own discernment. Call on your inner spiritual rebel and stop following the faithful crowd. A spiritual rebel is not naïve. Take people you might think are perfect off their pedestals. To do so means you will have to unplug from cultural beliefs that readily deify many public figures and leaders.

PRACTICE: Imperfection

1. Bring two of your personal imperfections to mind and accept them without criticism or emotion.

2. Picture five people who are in your immediate circle. In your mind give them permission to be imperfect also. Do so without judgment, without emotion.

3. Watch out that you don't compare yourself to them. Stay open; comparisons make us contract. We are shifting our everyday lens of perception from separation (contraction) towards unity (expansion).

4. Picture someone that you find difficult to tolerate over a long period of time. Accept their imperfection as a human attribute.

5. Shift into a full acceptance and realization that humanity is always in a state of imperfection.

Is there any such thing as perfection? Where can it be found? For me perfection depends on taste, appropriateness, and other subjective conditions. The temperature of the sea can be perfect for a swim. However, my perfect cup of tea could be distasteful to you. There is no enduring perfection when we use the personal or impersonal lenses of perception.

What about perfection without opposites? Is there absolute perfection? Yes. Absolute perfection, love, truth, joy, and beauty are all absolutes that can be experienced in the natural state. They are accessible to you in your spiritual nature. Withdraw your attention from phenomena, pull back in deeper than thought, and find out if you can access what shines from your innermost place. We experience the light that shines from the depth of our spiritual nature in absolutes. Perfection itself exists without people, objects, or experiences. Absolutes exist without being attributed to anything. Absolutes don't share the space with any other thing because absolutes are prior to separation and operate only where our unification or oneness lens of perception is activated.

PART 8

IT COMES TOGETHER IN THE END

CHAPTER 37

Free Will

Do you accept that every decision you have ever made was the only one you could have made at that time? If you readily agree, then it's likely that you already know or are close to recognizing that we don't have free will. If you don't agree, it's probable that you have a habit of harboring regrets about the decisions you have made in the past. If you are in the habit of regretting what you said—what you did or didn't do—you probably believe that you could have made a different choice.

Let's be objective. Imagine that it is possible to do a rerun of times in your life where you made big decisions that were not your wisest moves. Given the exact same circumstances today, would you make the same choices as you did first time around? If every detail was the same, yes, you would make the same decision. Why? Because a decision is the direct result of a blend of internal and external influences such as environment, people dynamics, emotions, genetics, body chemistry, mood, conditioning, and other factors coming together to give rise to your next move. How this complex blend of influences plays in each moment triggers your brain to connect neural circuitry in a particular way, and this connection ultimately dictates your choice. Your self-referencing network creates the thought that you personally arrived at a decision. And you did, but not in the way you imagined. Next comes the feeling of ownership of your decision and the separate self is validated. The DMN will judge whether the decisions were "good" or "bad." If our self-worth is low, we will run critical thoughts about our decisions and the habit of regretting gains momentum. If we have control issues, the pattern is exacerbated. Do you see the set-up? In any moment you do the best you can, given the influences at play.

The DMN overlays the natural flow of life with personal ownership, and we believe it and think we had and have free will. We reinforce the belief that we are separate, independent human beings. Our autonomy is born when we distance ourselves from believing we are who we think we are.

Can you see that you have always made the only decisions possible in any given moment, even when you thought you had choice? If you can't, it's likely you have a habit of harboring regrets. Regrets are personal "me" thoughts that vie for attention when you apply current day wisdom and hindsight to your past. Regrets make you feel bad. They present an ideal setup; a personal "me" thought coupled with emotional content. Regrets are a misuse of your emotional capacity. They are a symptom of a lack of self-love. They are a form of self-sabotage that gives rise to blame and shame, and there is nothing to be gained from them. The habit of giving attention to regrets promotes self-referencing which is the root of all suffering.

PRACTICE: Regrets

Divide a sheet of paper into two columns. Put the heading "Regrets" on one column and "Hindsights" on the other. Make a list of every regret that you can think of. Beside each entry, in the opposite column, identify and write down the blindspots you had at that time that poorly influenced your decisions. Your list of blind spots is a list of wisdom gems that you have gleaned from your experiences. Your wisdom gems are hindsights, and all you are going to take with you from what you have written down in this exercise. The experiences in your past are over; let them fade out now by loving yourself for doing the best you could have done. You did your best given who you were and what you had to support you at that time. Every move you made was good enough for life itself and it still is.

When your choices are not rich or laden with mind-consuming consequences it's easier to withdraw your viewing point from the phenomenal to a wider perspective. The wider viewing point helps you to recognize that free will is the result of a complexity of concepts taken to be true. There is no freedom in free will. Obedience to the workings of your neural circuitry is living life as a puppet to your conditioning.

Expand your perspective and see how the game of life works within you. When the personal perspective is running you will always appear to have free will whether you believe your personality is your true identity or not. Make the best choices you can in any moment. Be confident that that is the best you can do. The personal "I" sense stops there. Within the phenomenal world our choices have consequences, and consequences bring wisdom gems through hindsight. Be curious to find out what you can learn in the future about the decisions you make now.

CHAPTER 38

Control

In this chapter we will shine a light on control issues that can impede your experience of freedom. We will also identify the right use of control that will help guide your way.

Control issues are birthed from the personal "me" as a result of traumatic experiences. Do you have a desire to control your external circumstances? Do you have a fear of not having control? Do you spend time assessing threats and mitigating risk? Do you have emotional experiences where you feel you have no control? Do you respond to the impulse to have control over something and set about controlling your own body through eating habits, exercise, or obsessive behaviors? Do you spend lots of time assessing possible outcomes to your action plan so that you are able to meet every variation of outcome, making efforts to limit your public exposure or criticism from others? This is not an exhaustive list of control issues, but it is a good place to begin examining your own life and tendencies.

Your human life requires you to have a healthy inner-command so that you can live with some measure of balance. As your awareness of your personality's conditioning grows, your ability to self-reform increases. With a little bit of willingness, you learn how to manage your emotional nature. You learn how to manage reactions and reflexes that are consequences of believing personal "me" story thoughts. You can cultivate skills of discernment as emotional volatility decreases.

A healthy amount of self-control is established as your personality undergoes purification. Increased self-awareness makes purification happen. You become calm, less reactive, and inner contentment grows. Habits are broken and your attention is made available for what is happening in the present moment. You find balance between trusting the natural flow of life and your way of participating in it.

If you recognize a recurring need to control your emotions or the world around you, set about bringing clarity and understanding to your own patterns of behavior. The task ahead of everyone who is on the path toward spiritual freedom is to heal the wounded version of you who created controlling habits in order to survive and feel safe. Habits are softened when there is authentic compassion and love for the part of you that finds relief in control. No matter the route you take to resolve and heal, every modality will bring you to the potent remedy of self-love. If you let who you sometimes think you are come into the view of who you really are, a tsunami of pure love will hold, soothe, and heal you. If you have the ability to stand as pure consciousness, you will discover that every movement that emanates from it is loving. Not love *for* or love *because*, but *love itself*—unconditional love.

You are a multidimensional being who has the capacity to view life from within its story content. You also have the ability to perceive from viewpoints that are abstract layers of consciousness. Many can access the point of perception where it is recognized that we have no control at all, that we are being played by life itself, like puppets. From that perspective we see that our individual consciousness adds an overlay of interpretation where we believe that we create and direct our thoughts and actions. If you have not had this particular insight, it may seem very far out there. If it is, then it's ok to leave it out there.

When you pull back your vantage point, the experience is illuminating, similar to visiting a movie set during production. From the set, the fictional aspect of the movie is clear to you. Cameras, crew, lights, microphones, and actors confirm the unreality of the movie show during its construction. Seeing your own life as a long movie is a useful analogy. Spiritual glimpses and insights are when you have access to the backstage set. When you believe your thoughts, you are in the movie theater, you are the main actor, and you can easily be so locked in to the story that you forget you are in a theater at all. Wake up. The show is almost over.

CHAPTER 39

Nondenialism

Years ago, I woke up one morning, and my eyes opened wide. *Identification with pure consciousness has to go. All identification can be seen through.* With these words the solid ground of consciousness started to give way. Another major spiritual shift had begun. I knew that to abide in the awakened state one had to first get solid in one's true nature, and to learn how to live from there. Time helps our bodies and minds to adjust to new perspectives. It was my experience that shifting identification from the personal "me" to absolute, pure consciousness helps us anchor into an embodied awakening. I didn't know that there were other layers, deeper than an abiding awakening.

The phase beyond awakening is marked by three specific realizations.

1. The concept of identification is seen through. The urge to be anything at all dissolves.

2. The filter lens of space breaks down, much like the concept of time earlier on the path.

3. The concept of existence is recognized as myth.

What happens? Prior to consciousness happens. I don't have the vocabulary to speak about this or to this yet. As my perspectives reorganize themselves once again, "nondenialism" is a word I use to describe the experience of living prior to consciousness.

Nondenialism is the experience of fearless freedom in practice. Nondenialism does not negate the personal; no part of you is denied.

Your beautiful body and your personality are respected and honored. After all, together they make subjective experiencing possible. Nondenialism gives you the ability to see the full trajectory of your expression as divine, limited and unlimited, without identification. Subjective interpretations can happen and do not obscure, eclipse, nor deny the wider perspective. Life is lived in freedom where there is no loss and no gain attached to story. Your mind is picked up and set down, as needed, to participate and function in life.

Nondenialism is a way of being and engaging without denying any experience. Your position is open and available. You are empty and at the same time nothing is absent. Your viewpoint is from deeper than pure consciousness, and you are not attached. There are no preferences; no one lens is recognized as better than another. Your position is open and inclusive. Lenses of perception are tools for effective daily functioning. You are not attached to any viewpoint—personal, impersonal, unified, non-dual, nor pure consciousness. You can see how things appear as separate while everything is the same in essence. You can see the whole picture and the detail of everyday happenings simultaneously, without paradox or contradictions. Your position is deeper, and prior to the lens of perception that supports content. Every phenomena shows up according to the mechanisms of perception that you use to bring it into view.

In nondenialism, there is no mind play to include or exclude, to embrace or negate what is perceived. Your unlimited nature has the capacity to hold all perspectives, to accommodate a variety of different perceiving lenses at the same time. You can see how things are and how they are not at the same time. Each position is legitimate. One lens of perception doesn't cancel out or override another. Your viewpoint is so broad and inclusive that you can align with every position. A greater understanding of humanity is therefore cultivated. Because you are present and open, a willingness to help others replaces old habits of judging them. You know that in helping others, you are helping yourself in another form, because you now see separation and difference as secondary and useful only for day-to-day functioning. Everything and its opposite are both in view. This is possible only when you are on solid footing as emptiness with no agenda. Your response to life stems from a place without any agenda, from life itself.

In nondenialism your attention rests within. You are moved to communicate and to act from a place that is deeper than thought, personal beliefs, and habits. Yet, you can pick up your mind-body toolkit and participate in life. You will notice that your mind plays catch up, and its role changes from directing and controlling to supporting. You notice that speech and action are initiated from the stillness, not from a thought process with personal agenda.

Nondenialism is inclusive. It does not support dissociation. If you have hidden traumas, they will surface and seek exposure, acknowledgement, and healing. The practice of nondenialism encourages self-honesty. Your viewing point allows you to see habitual thoughts that vie for your attention. They don't stick; they can't hold your attention. Welcome new insights into the workings of your mind with courage. Don't get caught in any story. Celebrate that there is no place to hide. Do you respond to these words with either relief or fear? Relief signals a readiness to live outside of all stories, and fear indicates the desire to protect and control. An unobstructed view of the totality (the whole picture) includes an unobstructed view of you. Breathe away reactions. Nondenialism requires transparency and full honesty with yourself.

Is there someone in your life now or in your past with whom you feel totally relaxed? Have you had an experience of being totally at ease with someone, where whatever you say or do happens naturally, and you remain at ease? Perhaps the only time you experience freedom is when you engage in sports or the arts? Identify what gives you access to the sense of home within you. You don't need to route your access to your spiritual nature (home) through another persona or with activities. Our minds tell us we feel a certain way because of someone or something else. That's not true—our minds create associations to help us repeat what is safe—the associations are not the truth. Your mind has set up a circuit. Nobody or anything has the power to offer you access to your spiritual nature. Reclaim the potency to rest within yourself. Feel the autonomy knowing you have all you need within you. A spiritual rebel will feel empowerment as autonomy grows.

PRACTICE: Freedom with and without the Mind

Identify a moment in your life when you were totally at ease in your own skin, a time when you felt that everything was easy and natural. Tap into that experience using memory as a tool to access your inner "home," your spiritual nature. See if you can feel it again, right now. If you can, don't pay attention to the associations that mind makes. Rest within. What circumstances brought your attention there once has nothing to do with your ability to access it now. Claim your ability to rest there. You do not need your life to be a certain way for you to access what is your divine right and your divine nature.

CHAPTER 40

Truth for Its Own Sake

Truth will not show up as your experience when your attention is supporting a personal agenda. There is no space for truth when your neural pathways are running a personalized "me" story.

If you have yet to cultivate self-honesty and investigate within you, then your understanding about truth will be conceptual and your experience shallow. You will be attached to your idea of the truth, and you will refer to theory rather than to your own experience. The conditioned mind will want to bolster itself and gain something from knowing and living in truth. This is natural because the mind is self-serving by nature. The best you can get phenomenally is a life lived in fearless freedom. Truth itself does not engage in the game of life. Truth is only for its own sake.

Truth is fresh. Truth is in the moment. You can't plan to recognize truth within you tomorrow; it's now or not at all. Are you up for it? Will you live from the innermost sense within you? Are you willing to be open to fresh and new interpretations of what you perceive? You'll need to be present. Go ahead and get out of your head. Step out of your own way. Taste the freedom within you. Trust your words and actions that arise naturally when you rest inwardly. You'll trip up over and over again, and that's ok. Celebrate your imperfect humanity. Be happy that you are evolving, maturing, changing, and embracing life.

Live in fearless freedom by acting and speaking from the inner knowing, from Truth. Your role in the world doesn't need to be defined or modified by conditioned thoughts. Live without reference to your personal beliefs. How we function in the world is a reflection of our connection to our spiritual nature and is colored by the filter lenses of our human condition.

Freedom is an inside job. Let it shine from the inside out. Have your mind and your body be in service to it. Stop playing small. Truth has no familiar reference points; it doesn't have memory, and it doesn't repeat. To live from truth, you will have to set down what you know, and abandon your memories and expectations. Stop repeating mind patterns—every moment is fresh. Don't miss this moment; it's not a repeat of the last unless you drag memory with you. And now there is another new moment. Don't miss it. You don't need your brain to connect what is happening now with memories. Neither do you need to monitor or control the future by projecting personal expectations. How you have lived until now is what brought you here to the end of this book. Stop creating false perceptions from what is already known. Be without stories, interpretations, and controlling habits. Feel and taste freedom. Get out of your own way and let freedom express itself through you and as you, in the beautiful, phenomenal playground of life.

References

Fox, M. D., Raichle, M. E., et al. 2005. "From The Cover: The Human Brain is Intrinsically Organized into Dynamic, Anticorrelated Functional Networks." *Proceedings of the National Academy of Sciences*, 102(27), 9673–9678.

Doidge, Norman. 2007. *The Brain That Changes Itself: Stories of Personal Triumph from the Frontiers of Brain Science*. New York: Viking Penguin.

Raichle, M. E. 2010. "The Brain's Dark Energy." *Scientific American*, 302(3), 44-49.

Raichle, M. E., et al. 2001 "A Default Mode of Brain Function." *Proceedings of the National Academy of Sciences of the United States of America*, (98), 676–682.

Jac O'Keeffe experienced a spontaneous awakening in 1997. This gave her access to powerful, intuitive, and healing capacities, and influenced her change in career, from pioneering community arts policy at the national level in Ireland to opening a healing practice. She worked closely with a team of medical doctors researching the spiritual causes underpinning clinical depression. The findings culminated in a residential program that O'Keeffe developed, which successfully treated depression. In 2003, she left Ireland to deepen her spiritual practice. After a two-year period of no thoughts, the self-referencing mechanism that creates the sense of a personal "I" had dissolved. O'Keeffe began to work as a spiritual teacher in 2008. She now guides others in her teachings and publications in order to share what she has learned, and assists others to transcend both dual and nondual perspectives. She also prepares those who have had sustained spiritual awakenings for liberation.

MORE BOOKS for the SPIRITUAL SEEKER

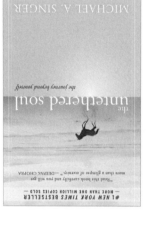

MICHAEL A. SINGER

the untethered soul
the journey beyond yourself

"Read this book carefully and you will get
more than a glimpse of eternity." —DEEPAK CHOPRA

— MORE THAN ONE MILLION COPIES SOLD —
#1 NEW YORK TIMES BESTSELLER

ISBN: 978-1572245372 | US $17.95

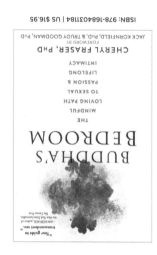

BUDDHA'S
BEDROOM

THE
MINDFUL
LOVING PATH
TO SEXUAL
PASSION &
LIFELONG
INTIMACY

CHERYL FRASER, PhD

FOREWORD BY
JACK KORNFIELD, PhD, & TRUDY GOODMAN, PhD

"Your guide to
transcendent sex."
—JAN KERNER, author of
the *New York Times* bestseller
She Comes First

ISBN: 978-1684031184 | US $16.95

EMPATH

I don't
want to
be an
anymore

How to reclaim your
power over emotional overload,
maintain boundaries &
live your best life

ORA NORTH

Foreword by
DANIELLE
DULSKY

ISBN: 978-1684034178 | US $16.95

THE
NO-SELF
HELP
BOOK

40 Reasons to
Get Over Your Self &
Find Peace of Mind

KATE GUSTIN, PhD
Foreword by JP SEARS

"Insightful, refreshing,
playful, and truly wise."
—James Baraz, cofounder of
Spirit Rock Meditation Center

ISBN: 978-1684032174 | US $16.95

newhar**binger**publications

⚙ NON-DUALITY PRESS | ⚙ REVEAL PRESS

Sign up *for* our spirituality e-newsletter:
newharbinger.com/join-us